HULLO...
MY NAME IS
ZIGGY
...WELCOME TO
MY WORLD

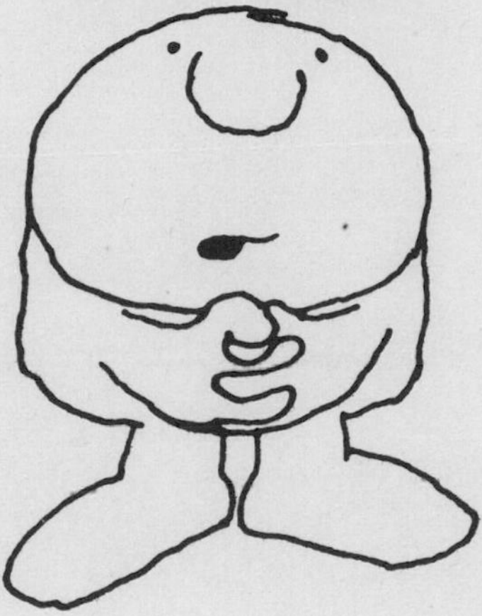

Life is just a bunch of Ziggys..

by Tom Wilson

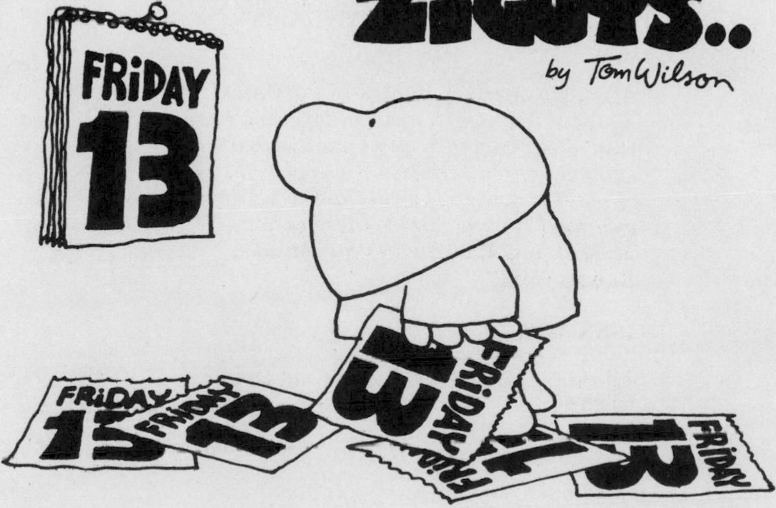
FRIDAY
13

Sheed Andrews and McMeel, Inc.
Subsidiary of Universal Press Syndicate
Kansas City

"Ziggy" is syndicated internationally by
UNIVERSAL PRESS SYNDICATE

ISBN: 0-8362-0551-0

Library of Congress Catalog Card Number:
77-93885

dedicated to YOU
...and all the other
ZIGGYS in the world..

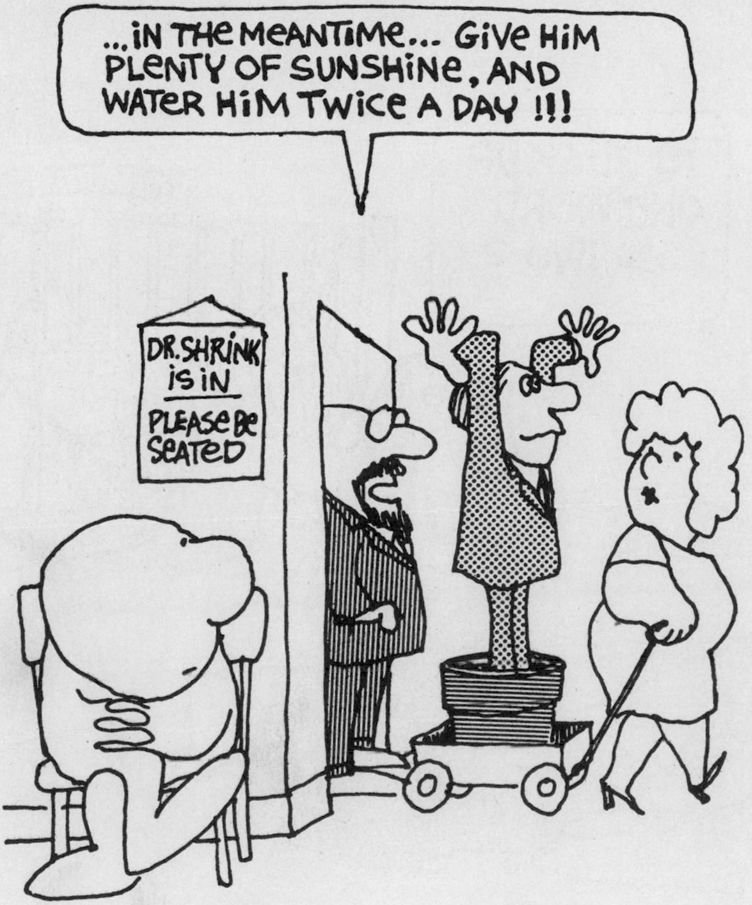
...IN THE MEANTIME... GIVE HIM PLENTY OF SUNSHINE, AND WATER HIM TWICE A DAY !!!
DR. SHRINK IS IN
PLEASE BE SEATED

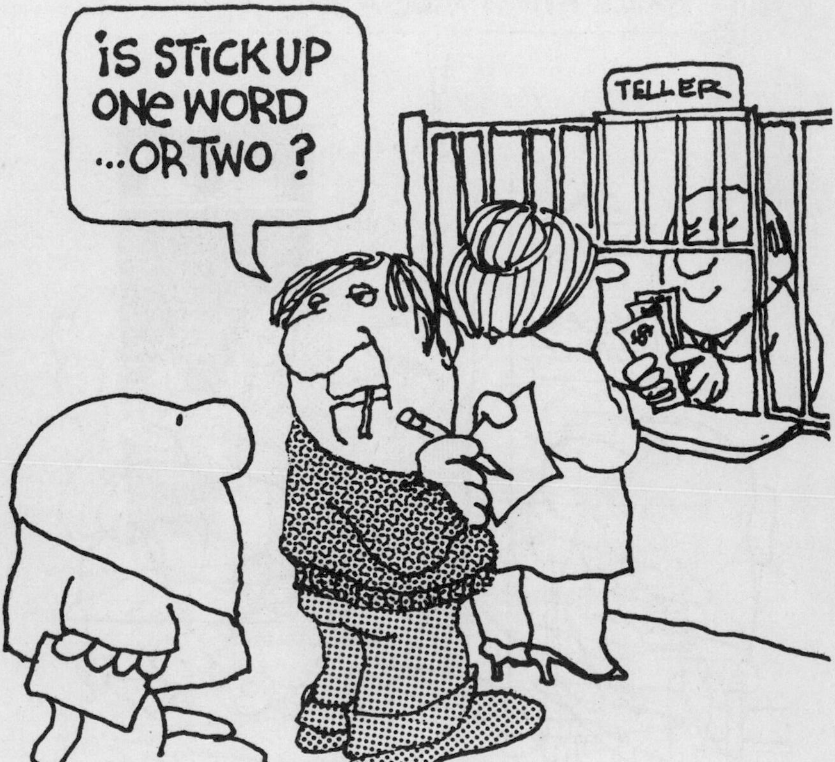
IS STICK UP ONE WORD ...OR TWO ?
TELLER

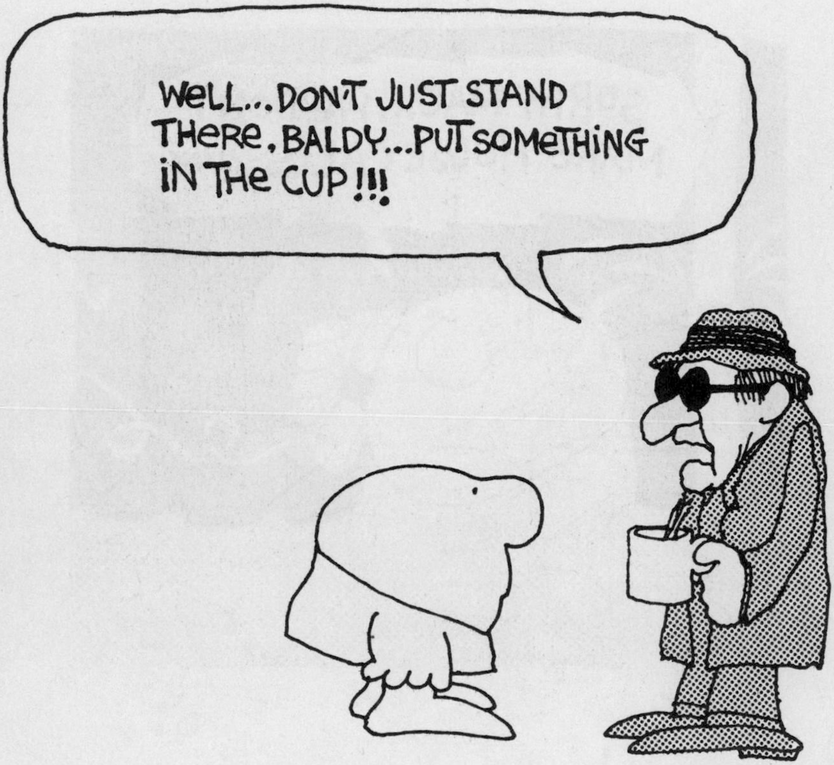
WeLL...DON'T JUST STAND THERe, BALDY...PUT SOMeTHiNG iN THe CUP!!!

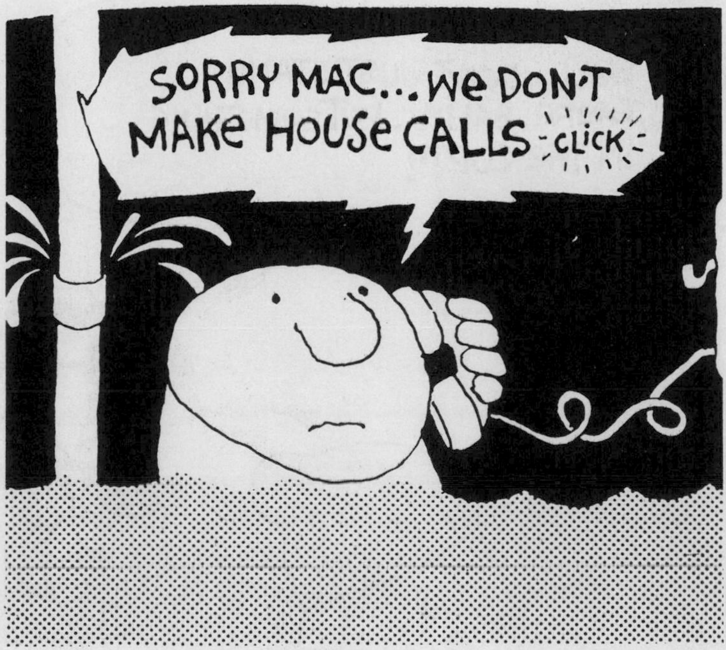
SORRY MAC...WE DON'T MAKE HOUSE CALLS
CLICK

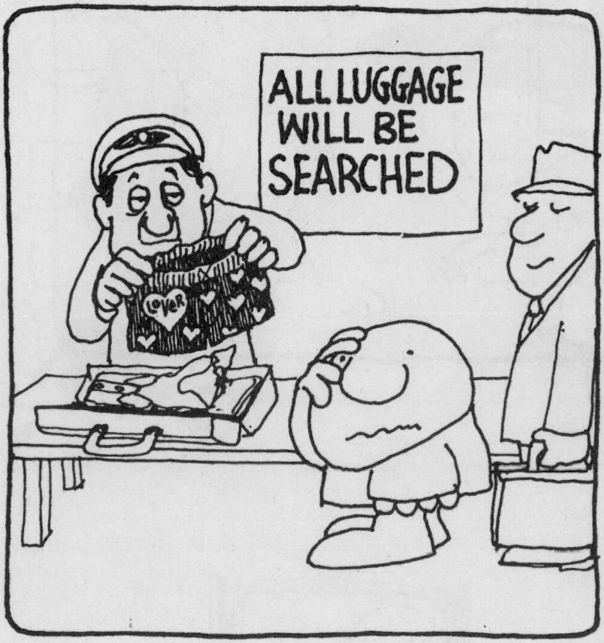
ALL LUGGAGE
WILL BE
SEARCHED
LOVER

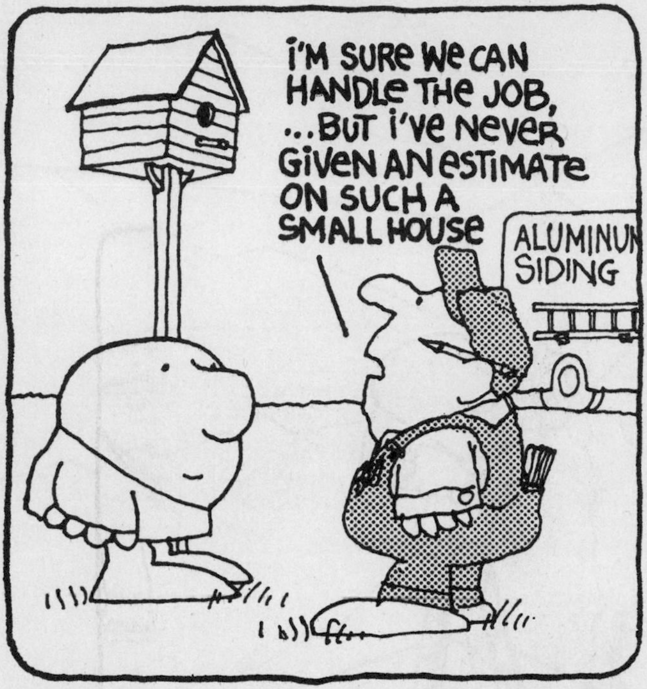
I'M SURE WE CAN HANDLE THE JOB, ...BUT I'VE NEVER GIVEN AN ESTIMATE ON SUCH A SMALL HOUSE
ALUMINUM
SIDING

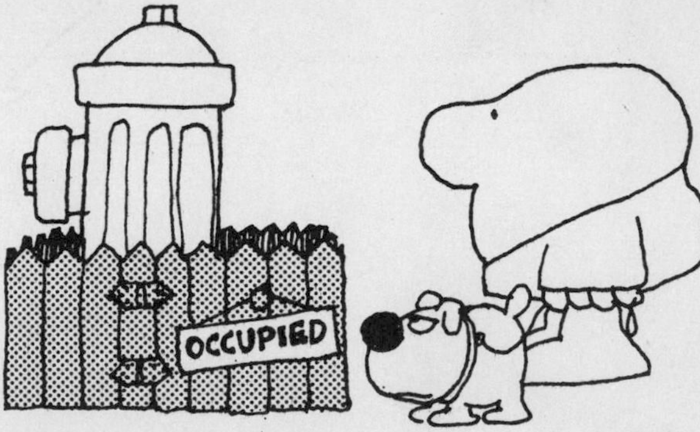
OCCUPIED

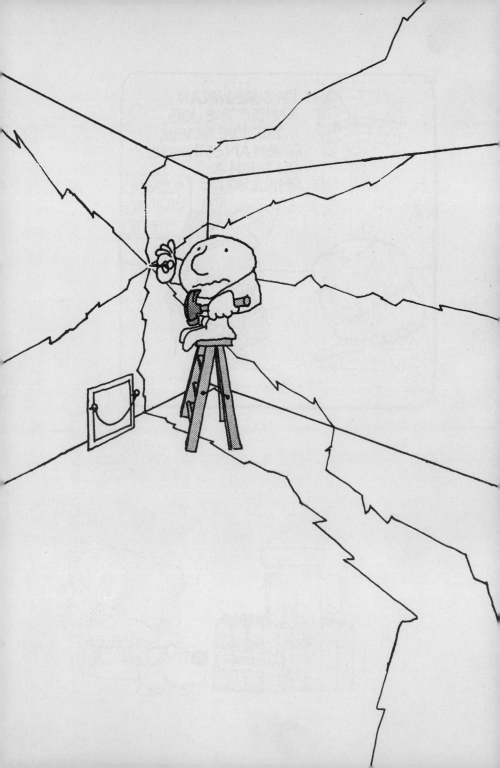

A.B.C.
CHILDREN'S
BOOK CO.

OUT
TO
DiN-DiN

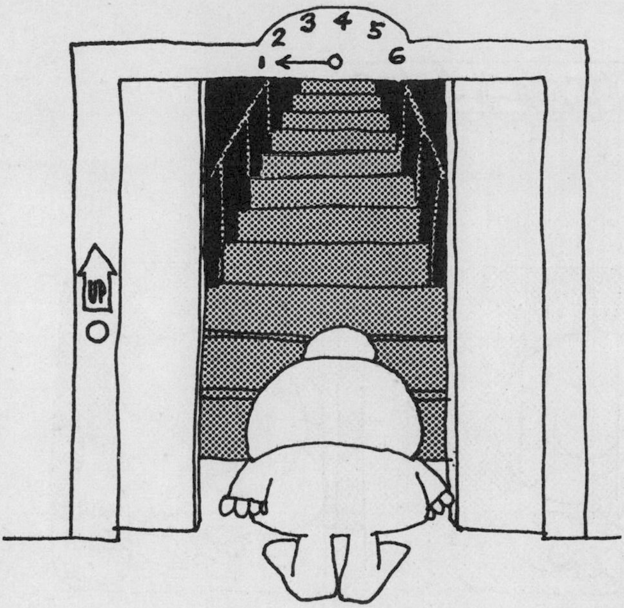
2 3 4 5
1 6
UP

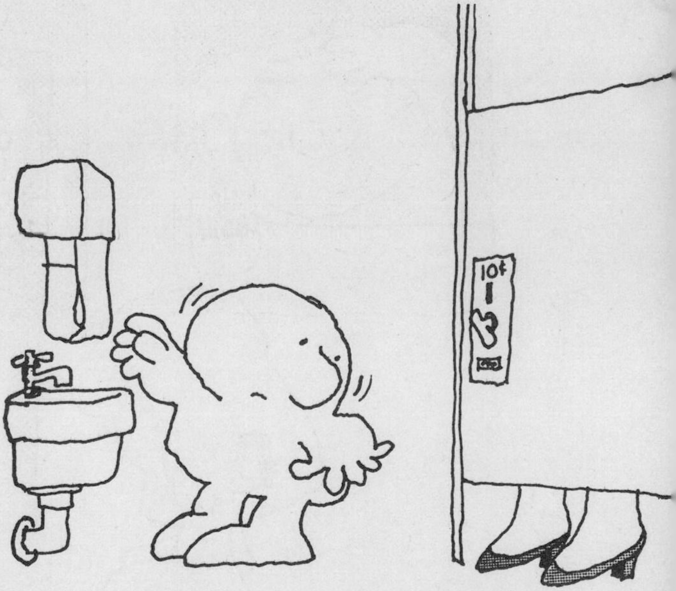
10¢

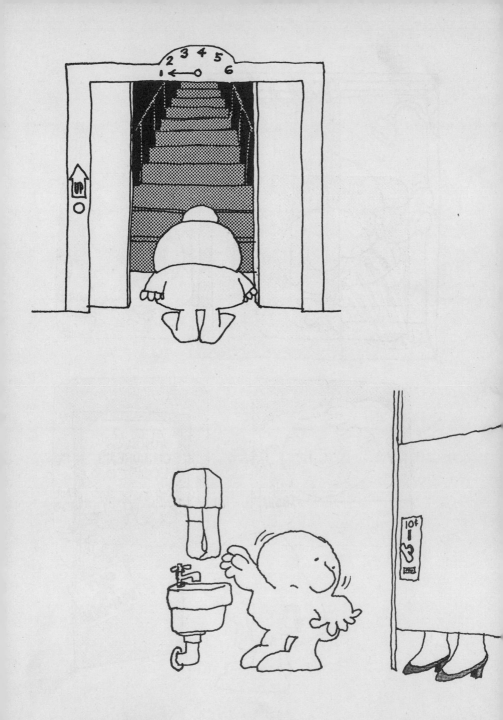

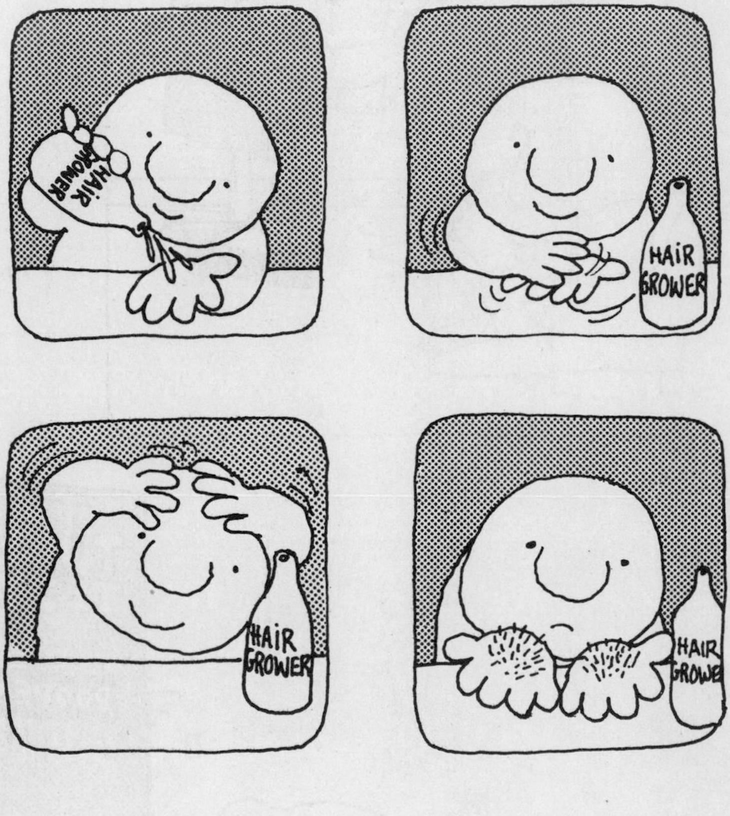
HAIR GROWER
HAIR GROWER
HAIR GROWER
HAIR GROWE

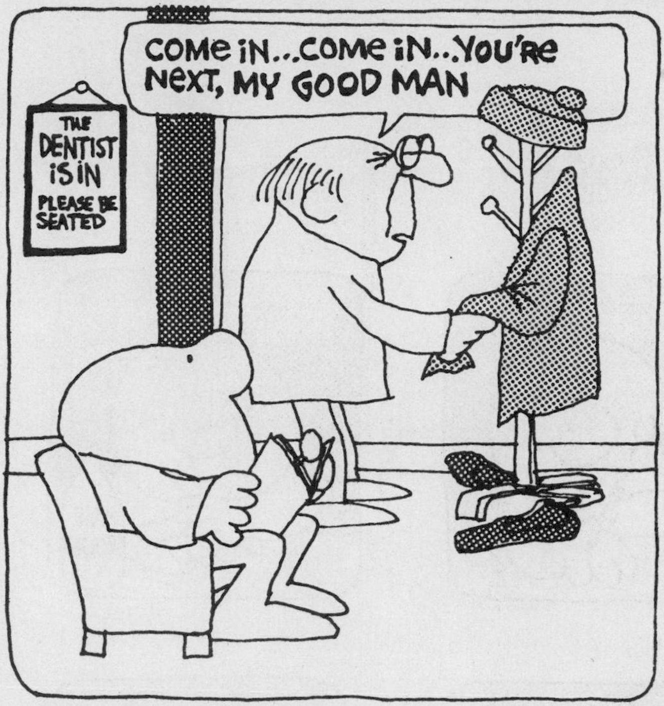
COME IN...COME IN...YOU'RE NEXT, MY GOOD MAN
THE DENTIST IS IN PLEASE BE SEATED

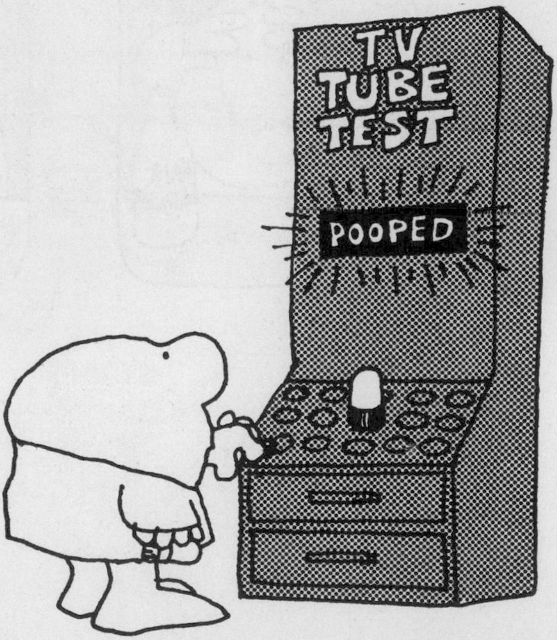
TV TUBE TEST
POOPED

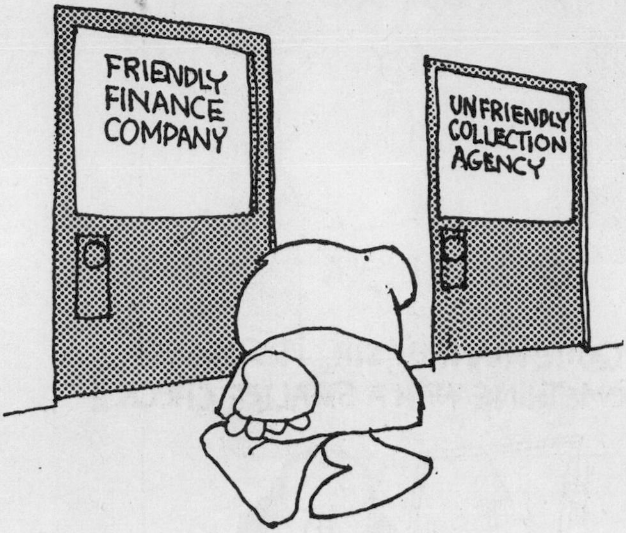
FRIENDLY FINANCE COMPANY
UNFRIENDLY COLLECTION AGENCY

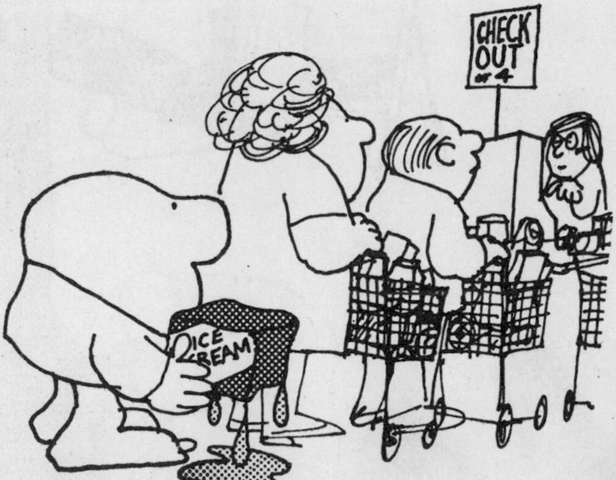
CHECK OUT #4
ICE CREAM

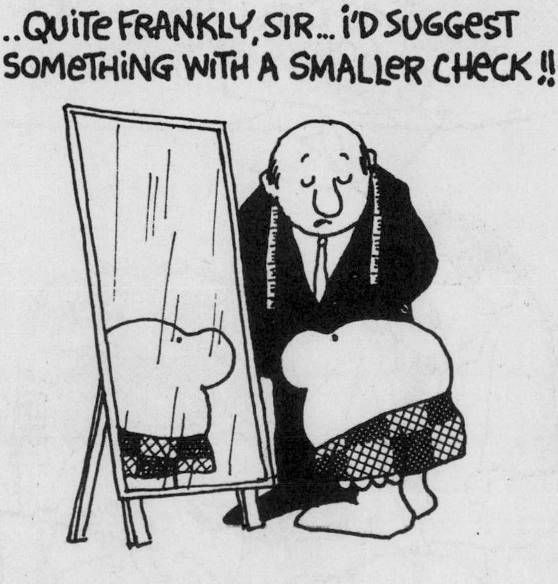
..QUITE FRANKLY, SIR... I'D SUGGEST SOMETHING WITH A SMALLER CHECK !!

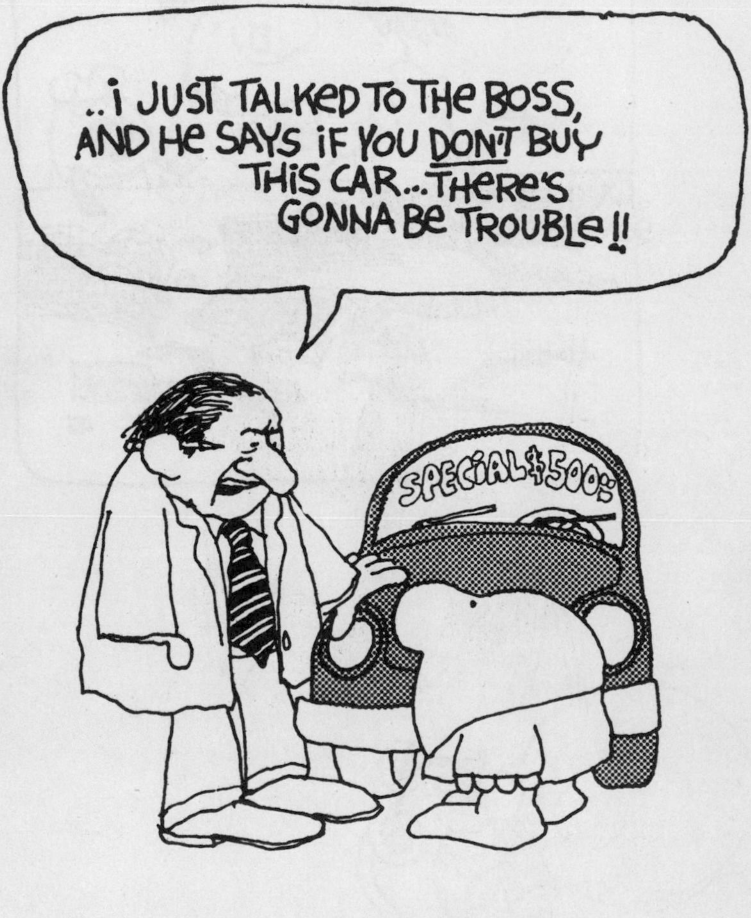
..i JUST TALKED TO THE BOSS, AND HE SAYS iF YOU DON'T BUY THIS CAR...THERE'S GONNA BE TROUBLE!!
SPECIAL $500.00

IN YOUR CASE I WOULD RECOMMEND THE MODEL OVER HERE WITH THE EMERGENCY SHUT-OFF SWITCH
APPLIANCES

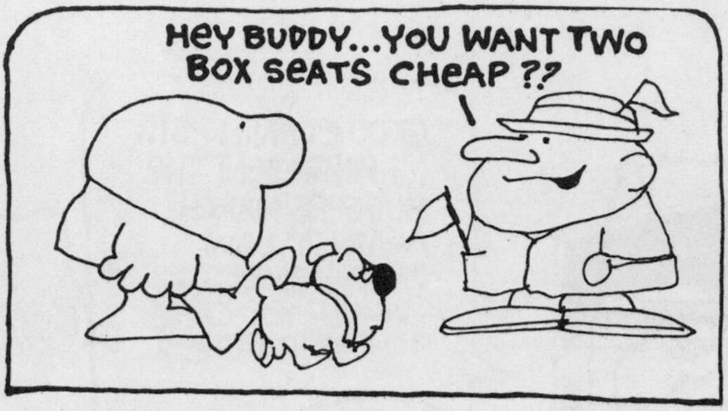
HEY BUDDY...YOU WANT TWO BOX SEATS CHEAP ??

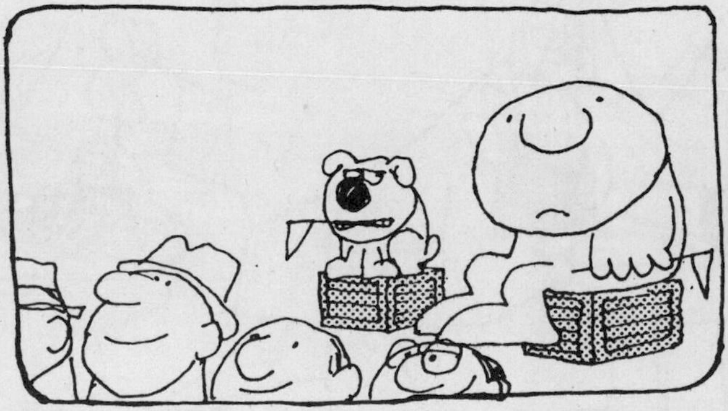

GOOD EVENING, SIR ..I REPRESENT THE MUGGERS' MARCH AGAINST LAW ENFORCEMENT... ..WOULD YOU CARE TO CONTRIBUTE?

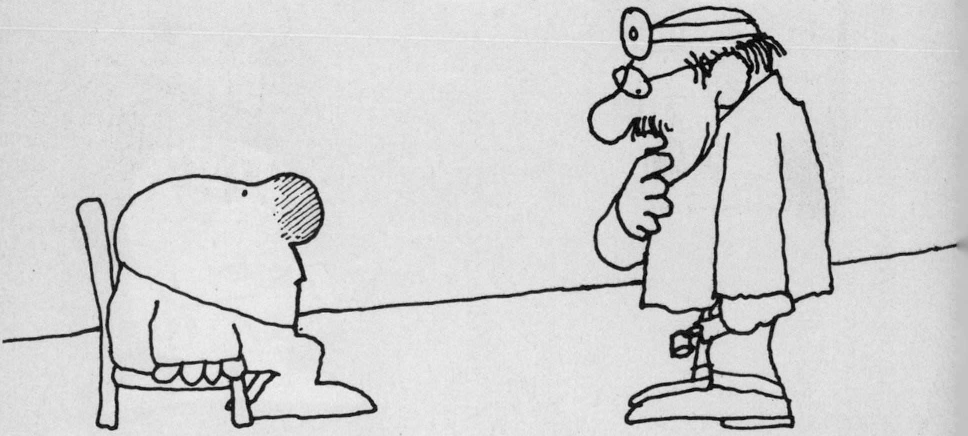

...ONLY CASE ON RECORD
MR. ZIGGY, YOU'RE ALLERGIC
TO FOUR-LEAF CLOVER....

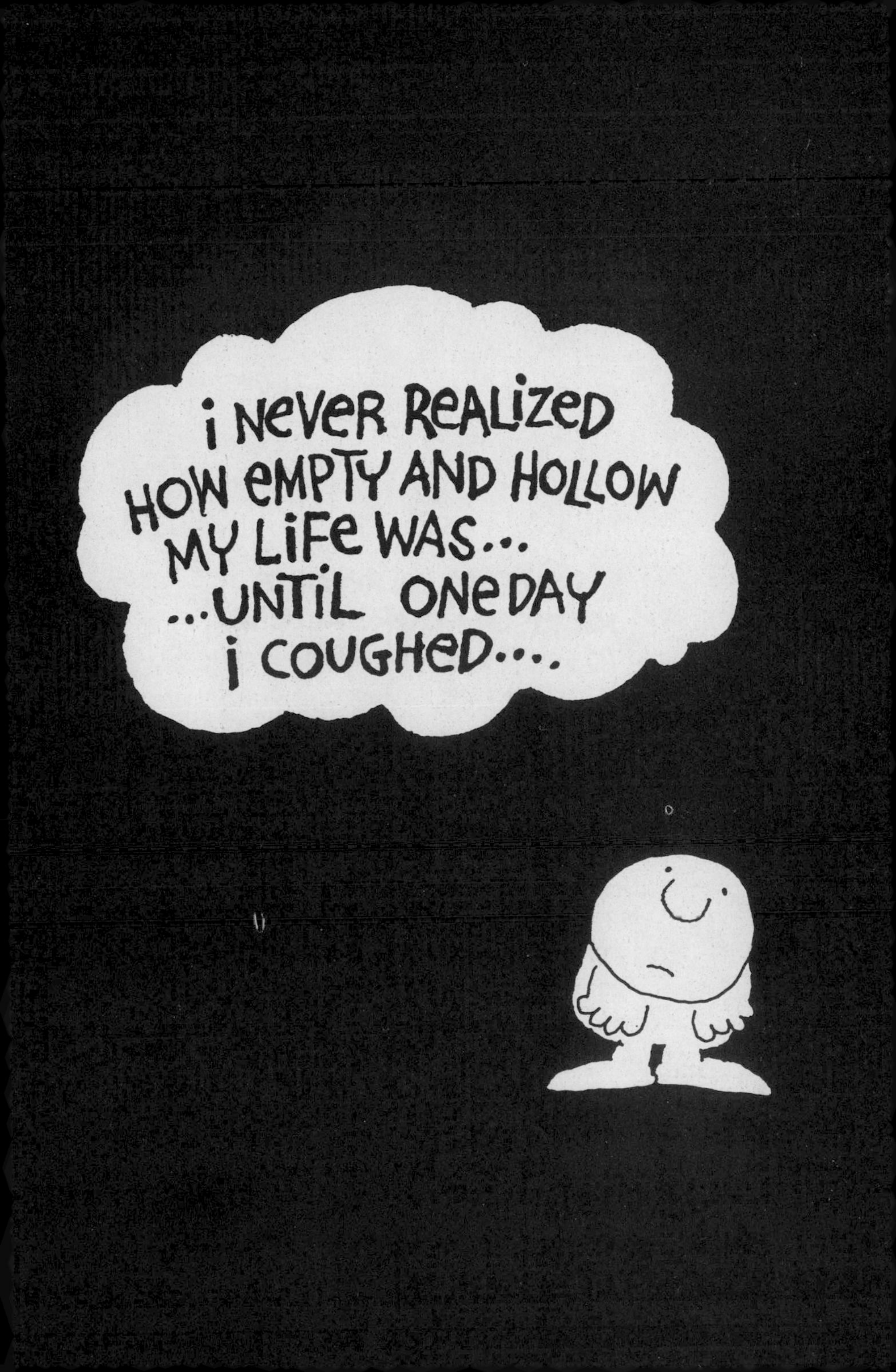
i NeVER REALIZED HOW eMPTY AND HOLLOW MY LIFe WAS... ...UNTIL ONe DAY i COUGHeD....

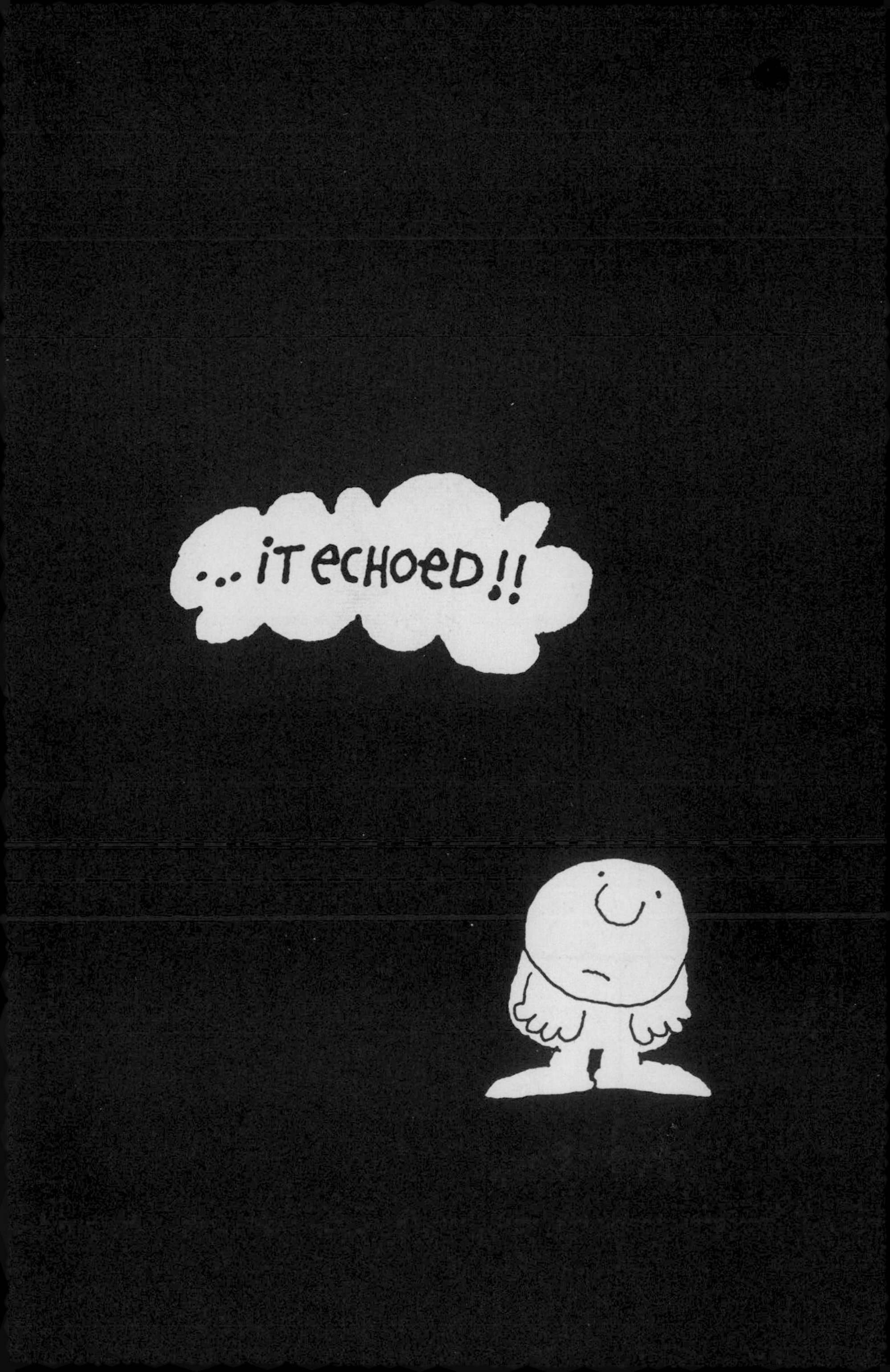
...it echoed!!

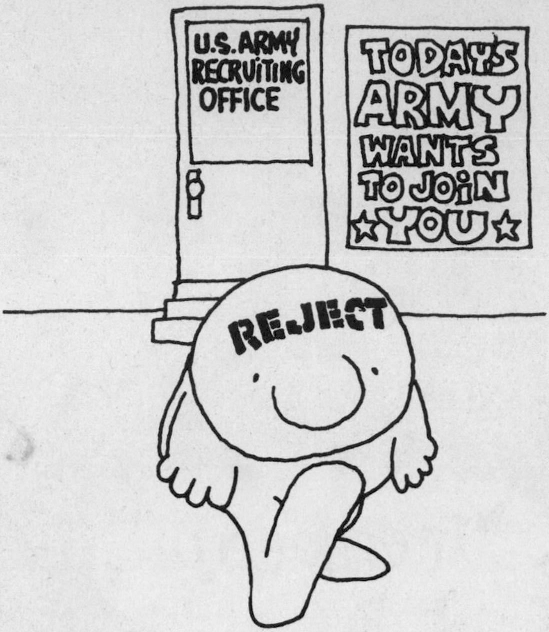
U.S. ARMY
RECRUITING
OFFICE
TODAYS
ARMY
WANTS
TO JOIN
YOU
REJECT

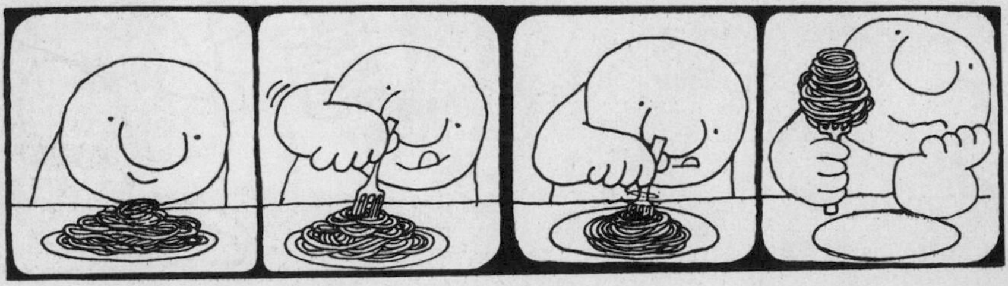

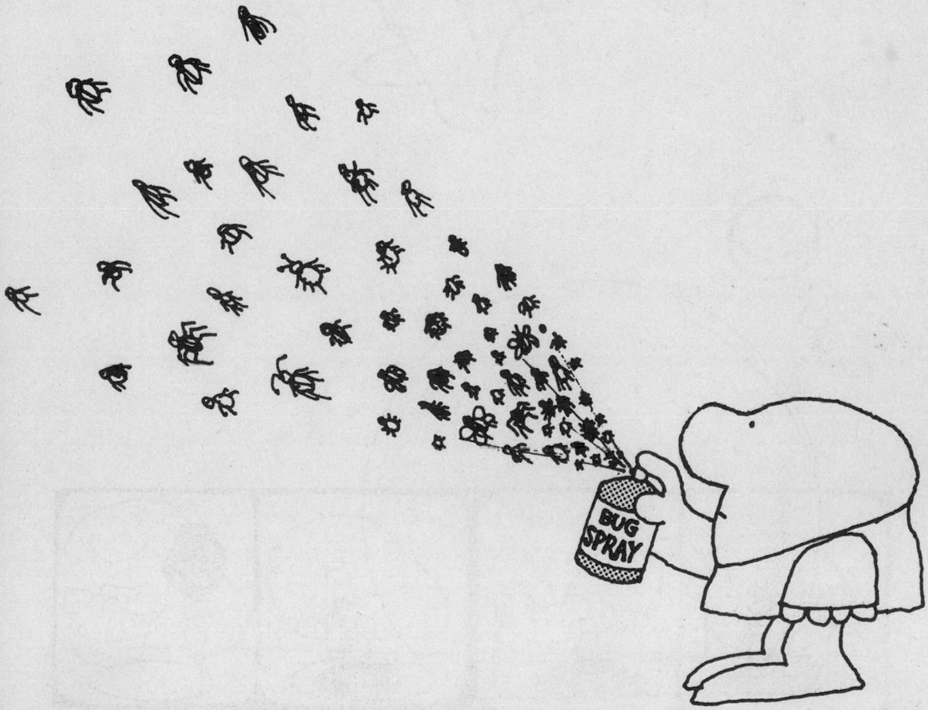
BUG
SPRAY

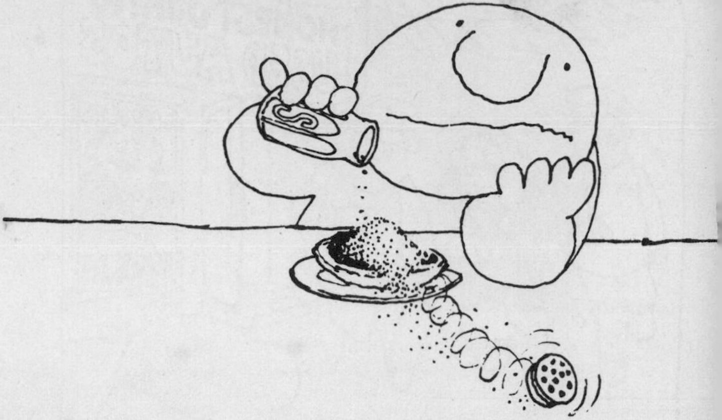

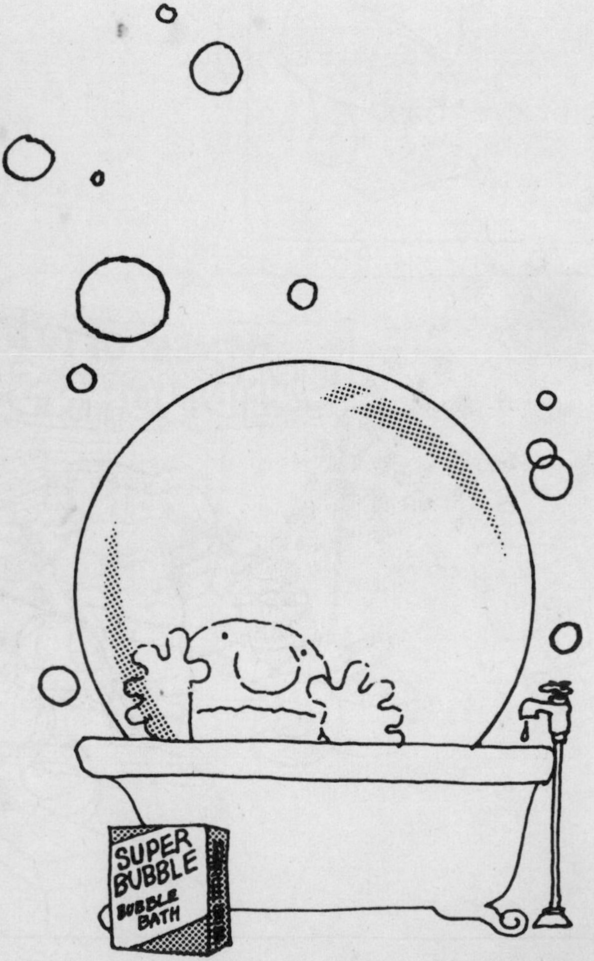
SUPER BUBBLE
BUBBLE BATH

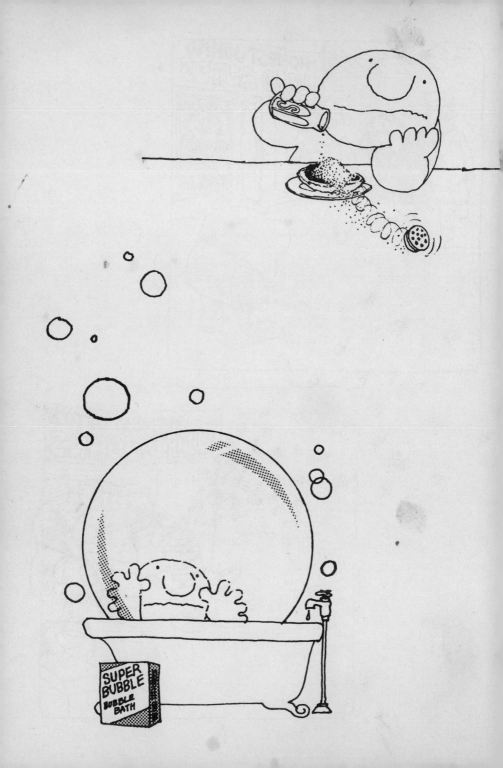

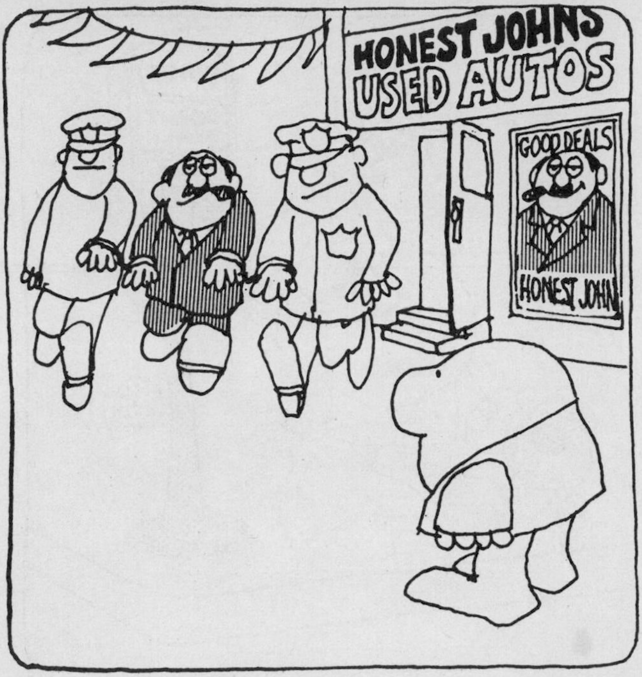
HONEST JOHNS
USED AUTOS
GOOD DEALS
HONEST JOHN

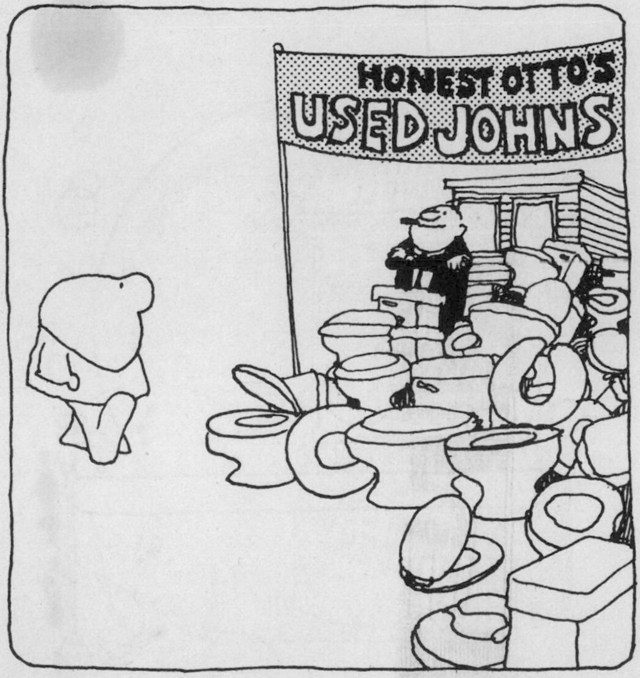
HONEST OTTO'S
USED JOHNS

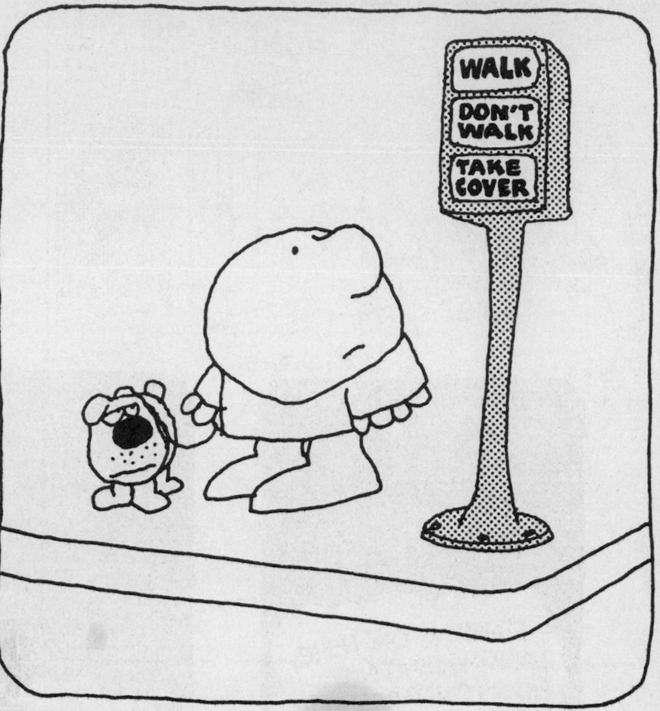
WALK
DON'T WALK
TAKE COVER

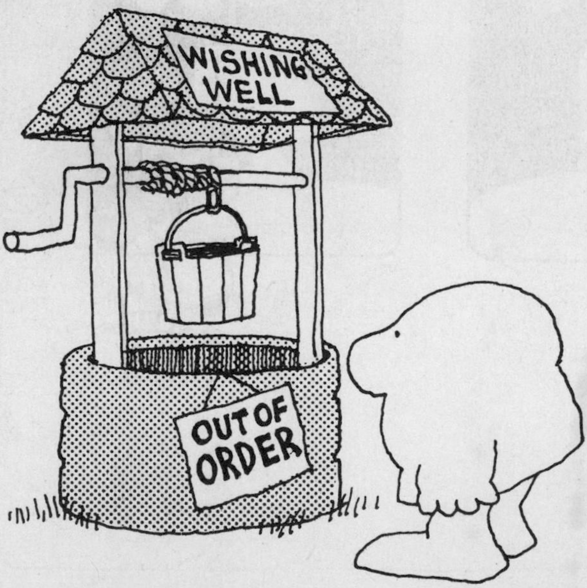
WISHING WELL
OUT OF ORDER

STANDING OUT HERE, LOOKING UP AT THE STARS CERTAINLY MAKES A PERSON FEEL SMALL AND INSIGNIFICANT!
...I CAN DO WITHOUT THAT!

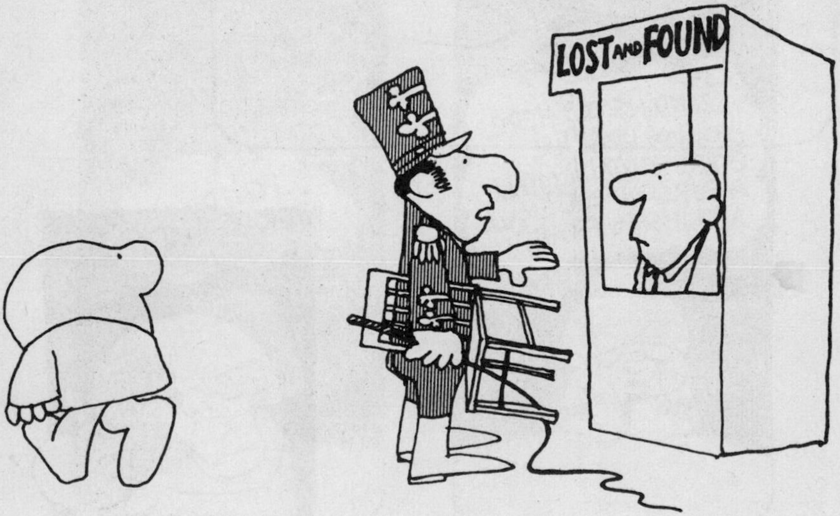
LOST AND FOUND

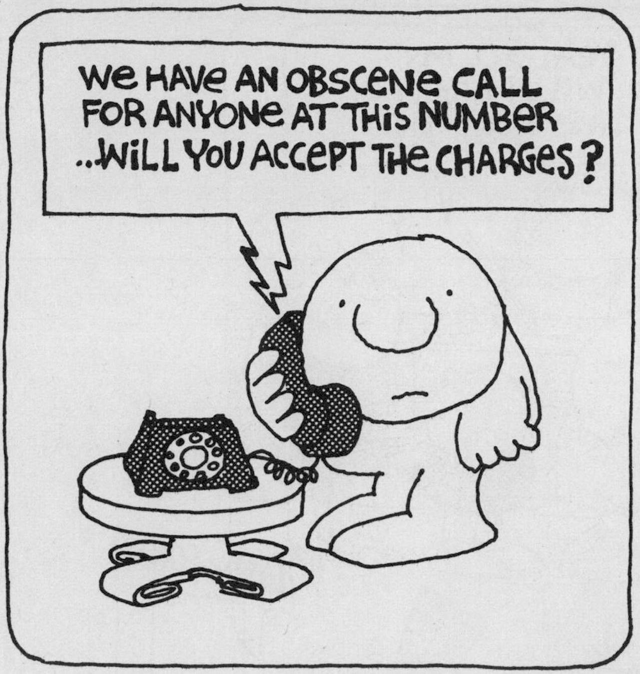
WE HAVE AN OBSCENE CALL FOR ANYONE AT THIS NUMBER ..WILL YOU ACCEPT THE CHARGES ?

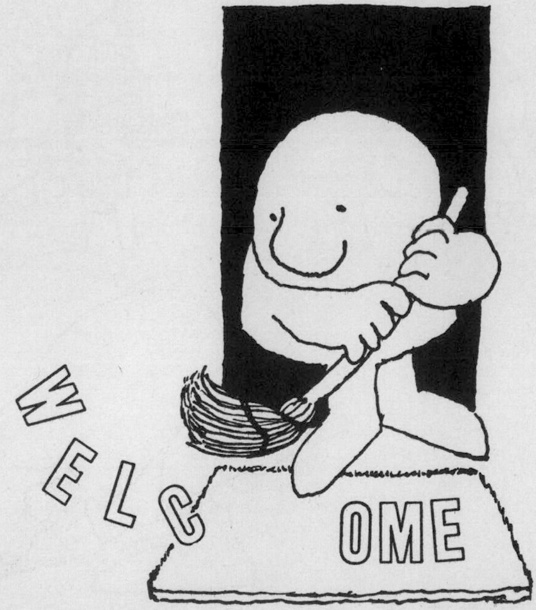
W E L C OME

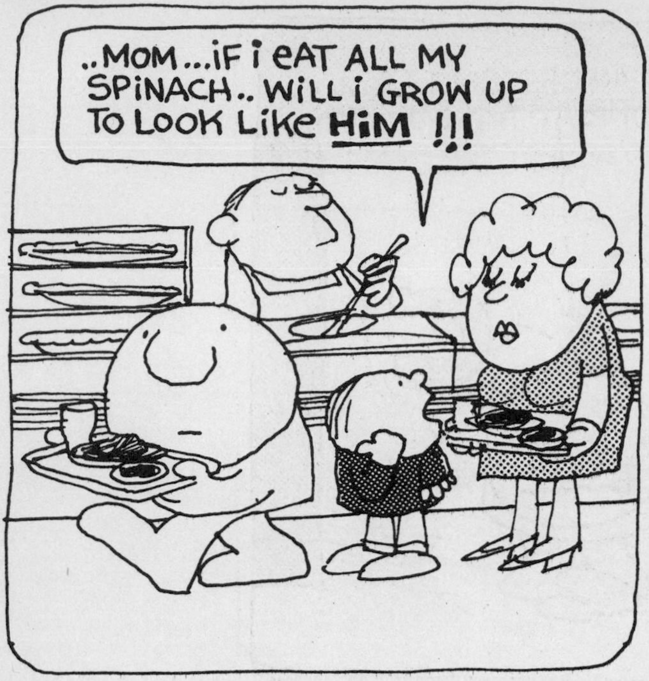
..MOM...iF i eAT ALL MY SPiNACH.. WiLL i GROW UP TO LOOK LiKe HiM !!!

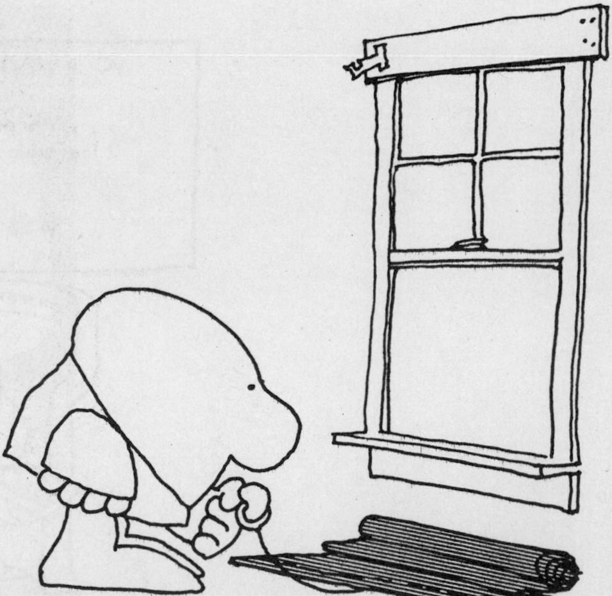

YOUR WEIGHT AND FORTUNE

. . . You are 3 feet tall,
2 feet wide and weigh 42 pounds

. . . YOU NEED HELP!

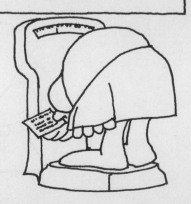

EVERY ZIGGY NEEDS a FrIEND

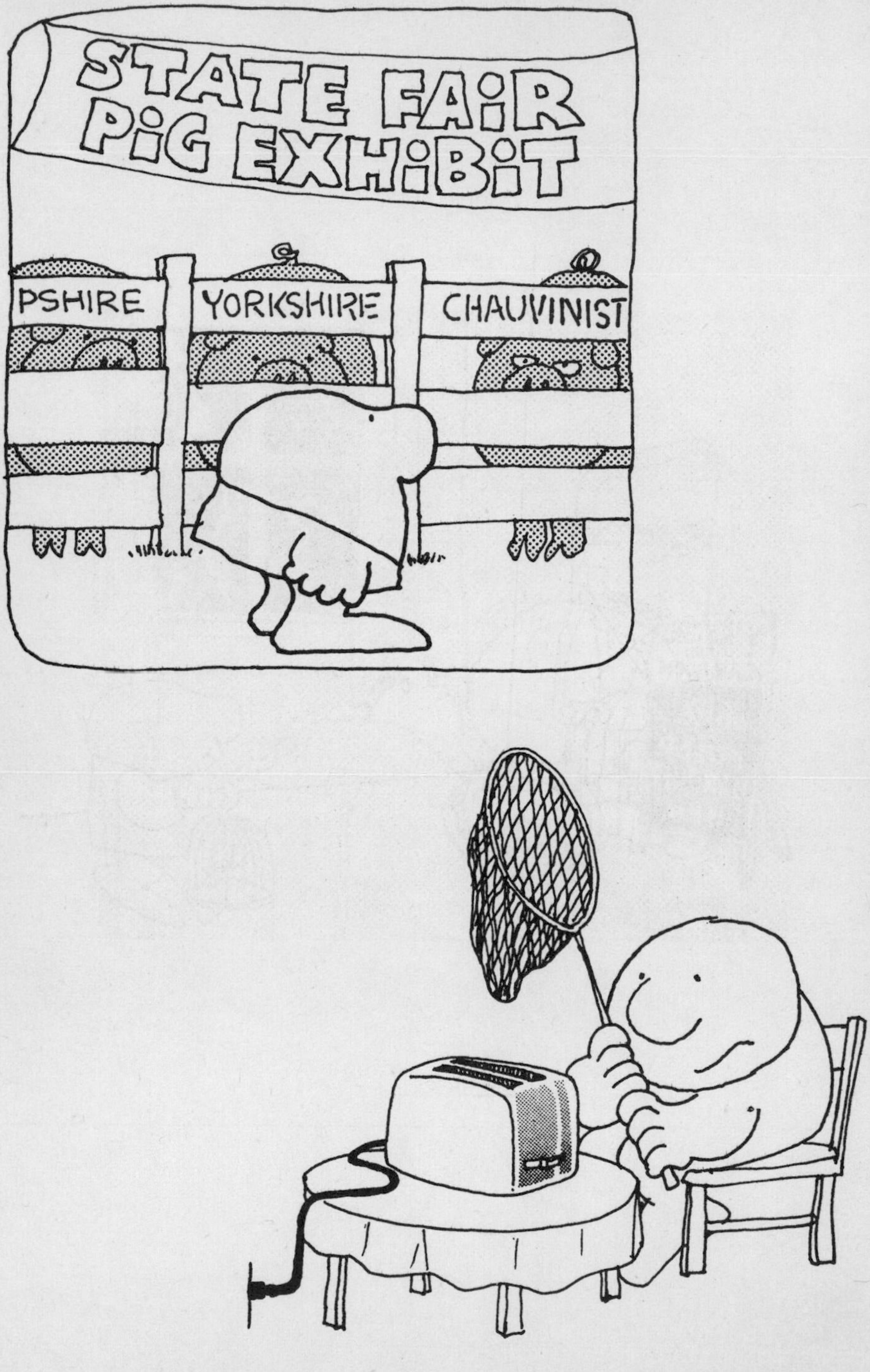
STATE FAIR
PIG EXHIBIT
PSHIRE
YORKSHIRE
CHAUVINIST

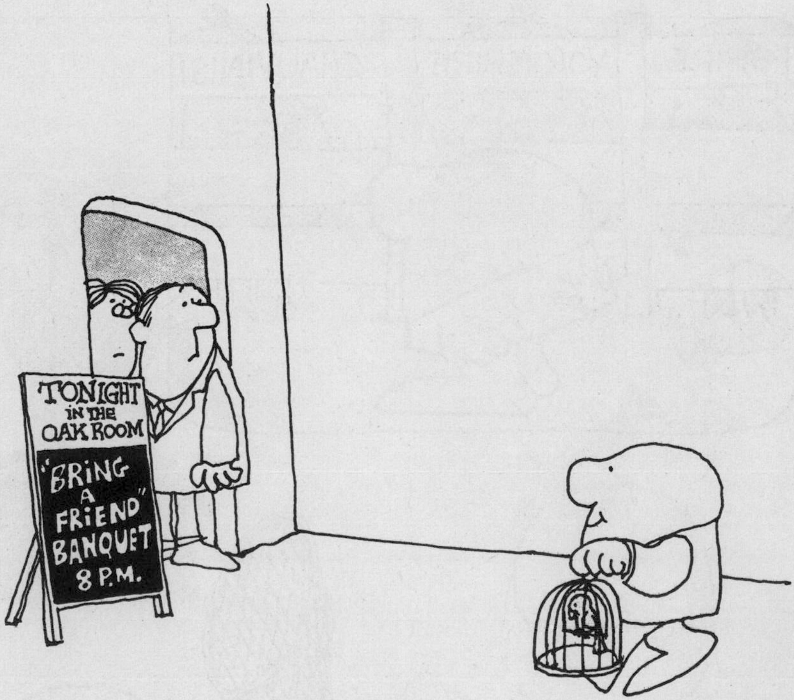
TONIGHT
IN THE
OAK ROOM
"BRING
A
FRIEND"
BANQUET
8 P.M.

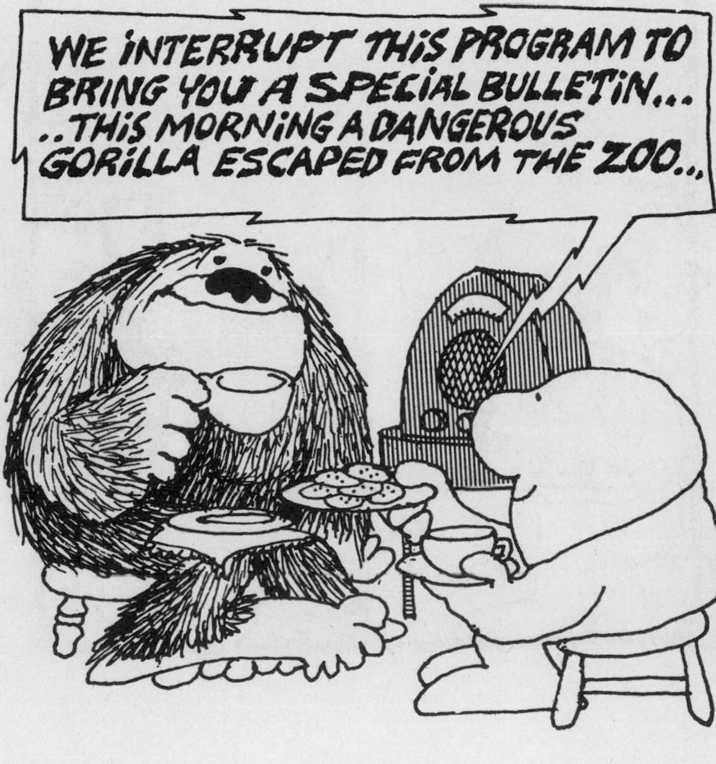
WE INTERRUPT THIS PROGRAM TO BRING YOU A SPECIAL BULLETIN... ..THIS MORNING A DANGEROUS GORILLA ESCAPED FROM THE ZOO..,

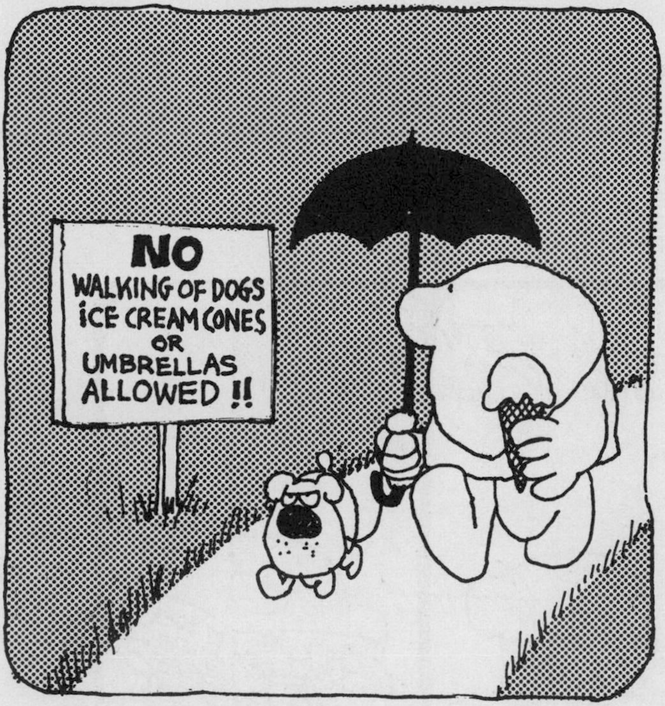
NO
WALKING OF DOGS
ICE CREAM CONES
OR
UMBRELLAS
ALLOWED !!

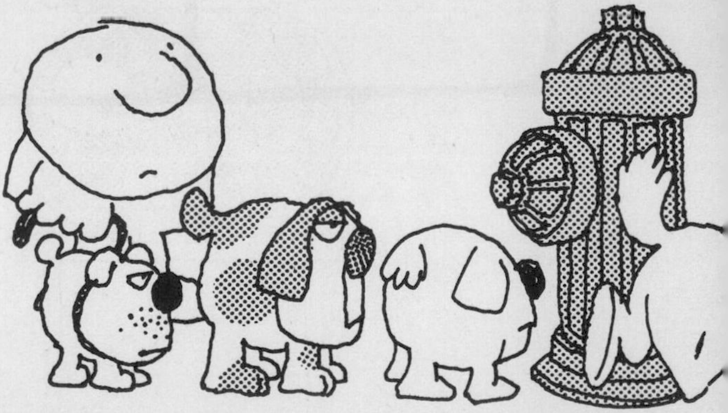

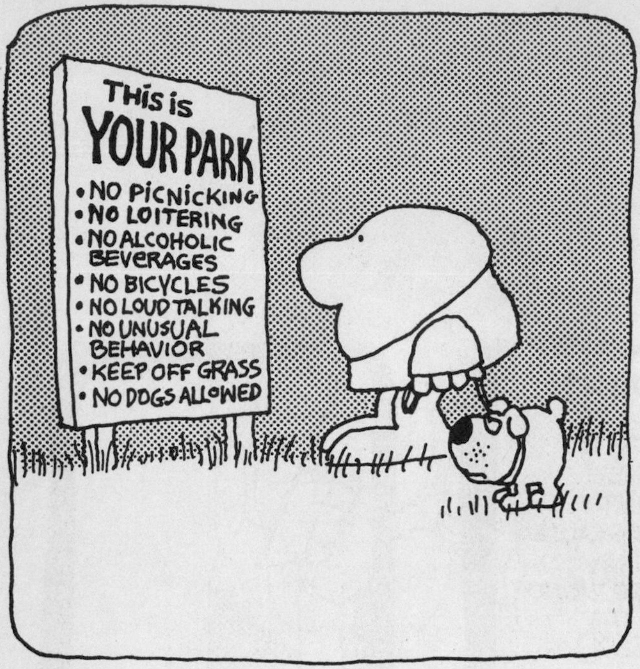
This is
YOUR PARK
• NO PICNICKING
• NO LOITERING
• NO ALCOHOLIC BEVERAGES
• NO BICYCLES
• NO LOUD TALKING
• NO UNUSUAL BEHAVIOR
• KEEP OFF GRASS
• NO DOGS ALLOWED

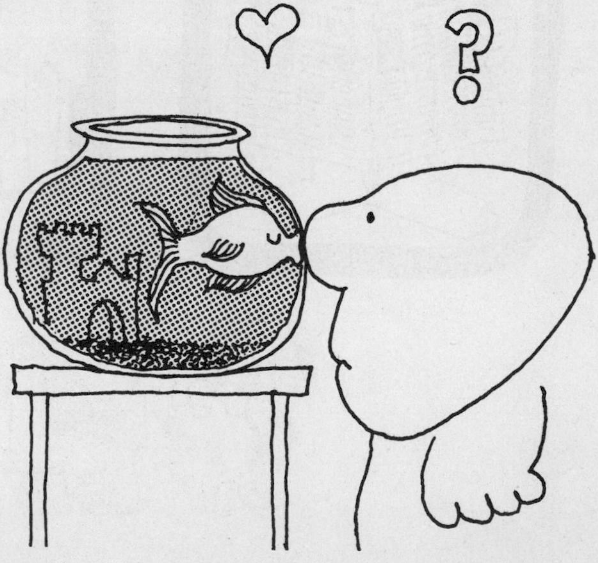

—YOUR HOROSCOPE—

BE PREPARED TO WELCOME A NEW COMPANION INTO YOUR LIFE BECAUSE TODAY YOU MAY MEET A CUTE BLONDE MEMBER OF THE OPPOSITE SEX

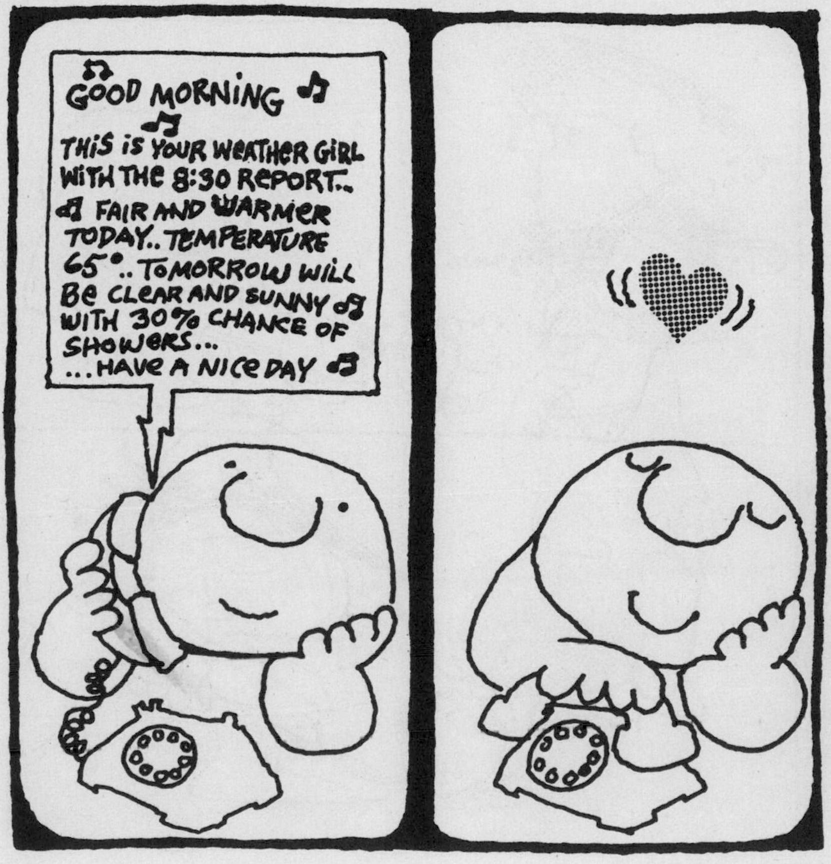
GOOD MORNING
THIS IS YOUR WEATHER GIRL WITH THE 8:30 REPORT.. FAIR AND WARMER TODAY.. TEMPERATURE 65°.. TOMORROW WILL BE CLEAR AND SUNNY WITH 30% CHANCE OF SHOWERS... ...HAVE A NICE DAY

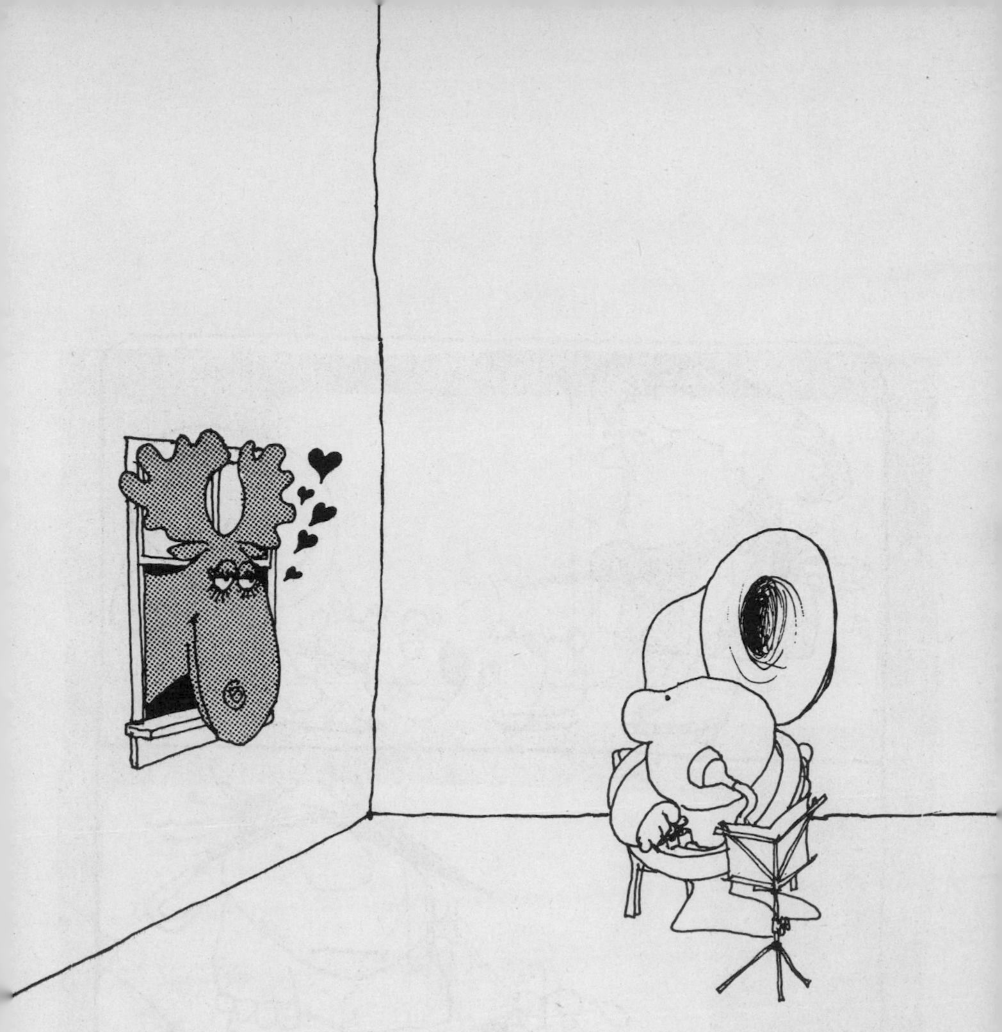

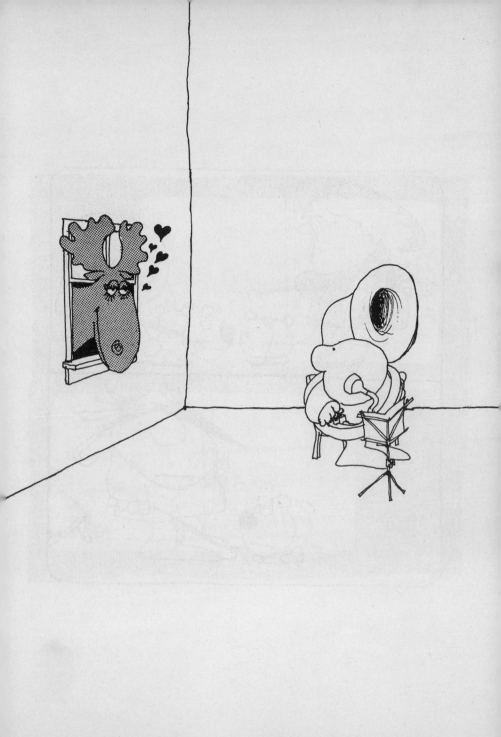

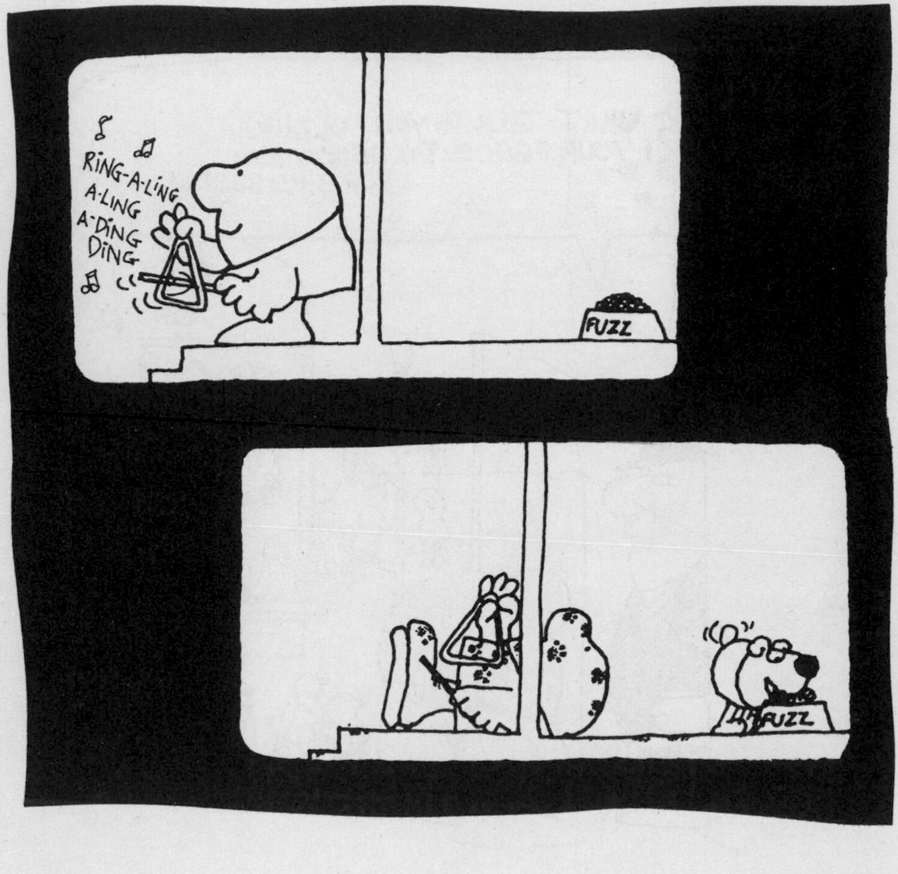

RING-A-LING
A-LING
A-DING
DING
FUZZ
FUZZ

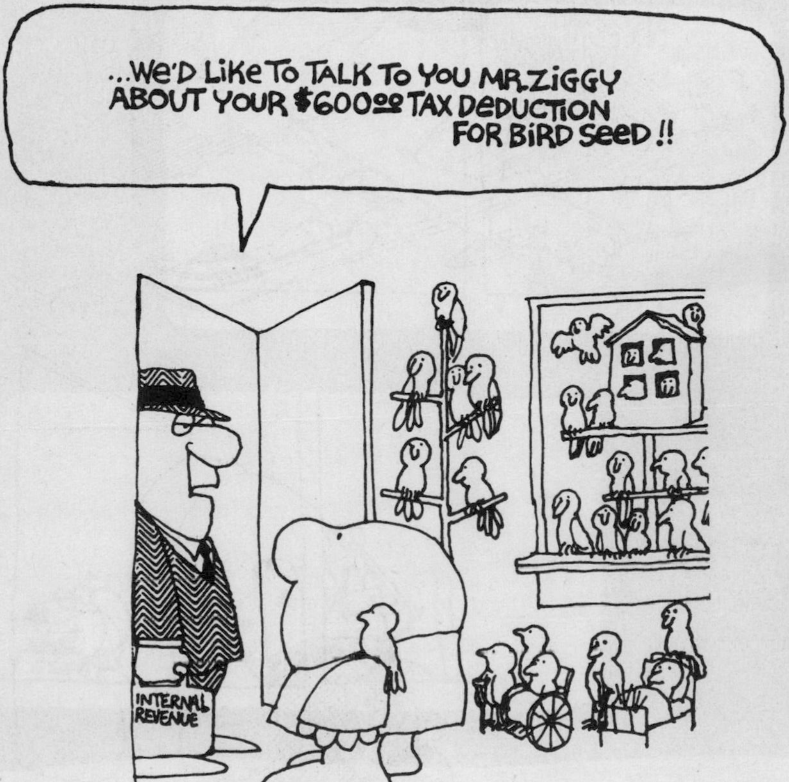
...WE'D LIKE TO TALK TO YOU MR. ZIGGY ABOUT YOUR $600.00 TAX DEDUCTION FOR BIRD SEED!!
INTERNAL REVENUE

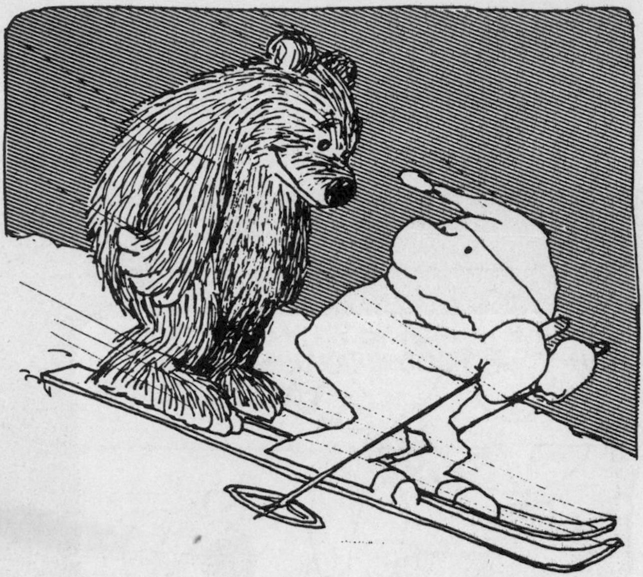

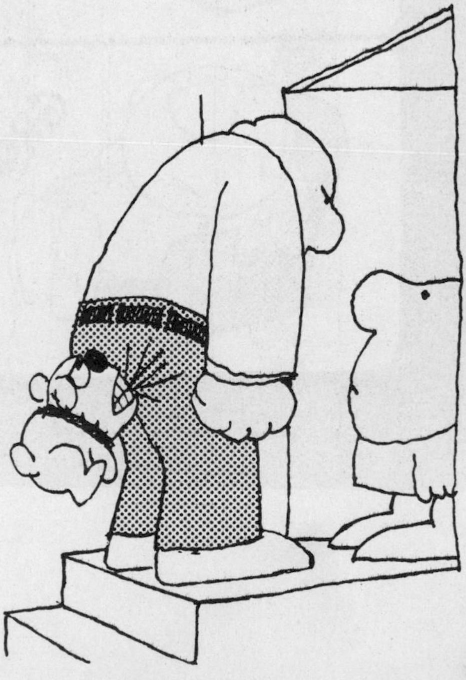

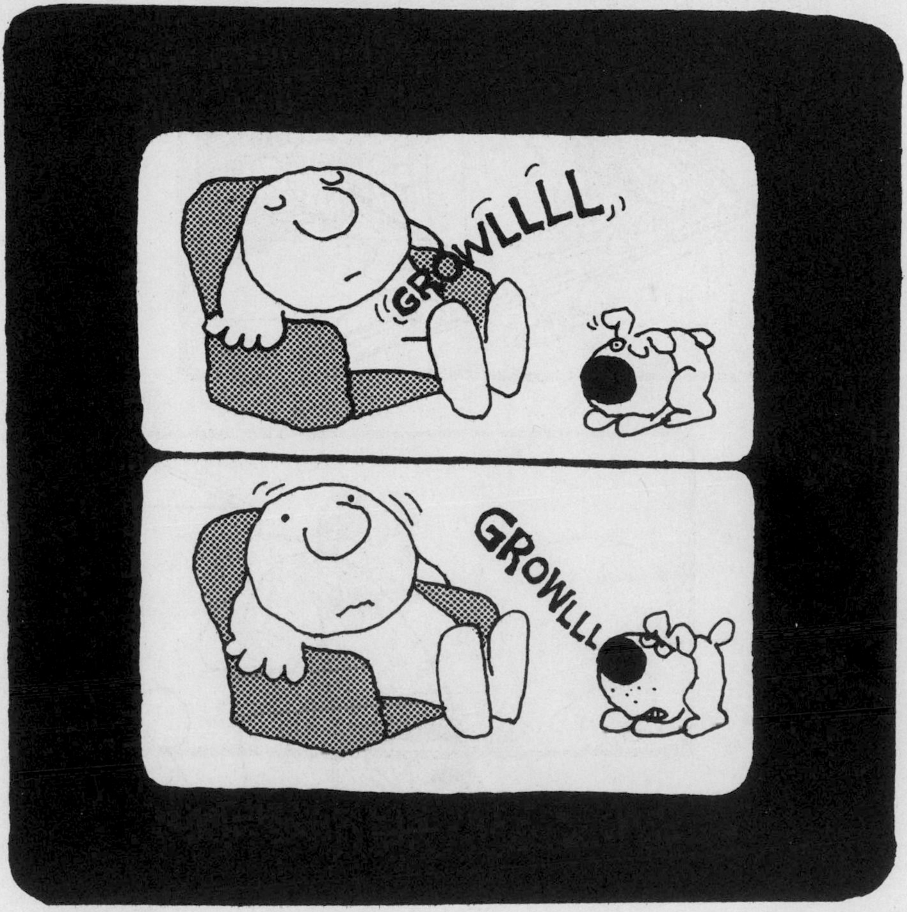
GROWLLLLL
GROWLLL

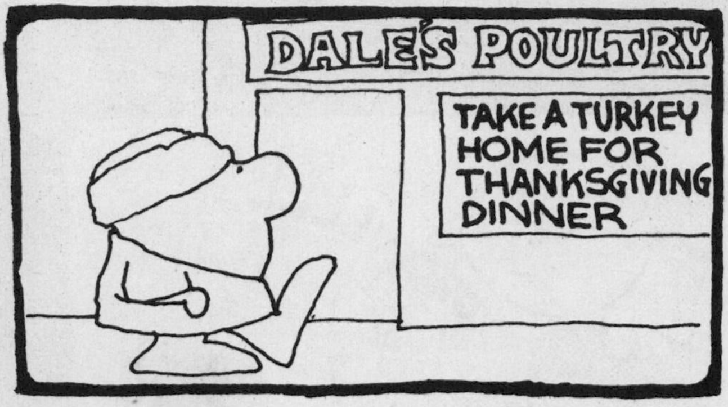
DALE'S POULTRY
TAKE A TURKEY HOME FOR THANKSGIVING DINNER

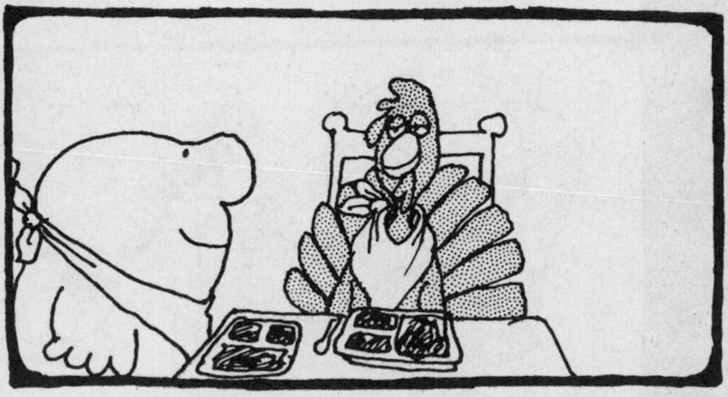

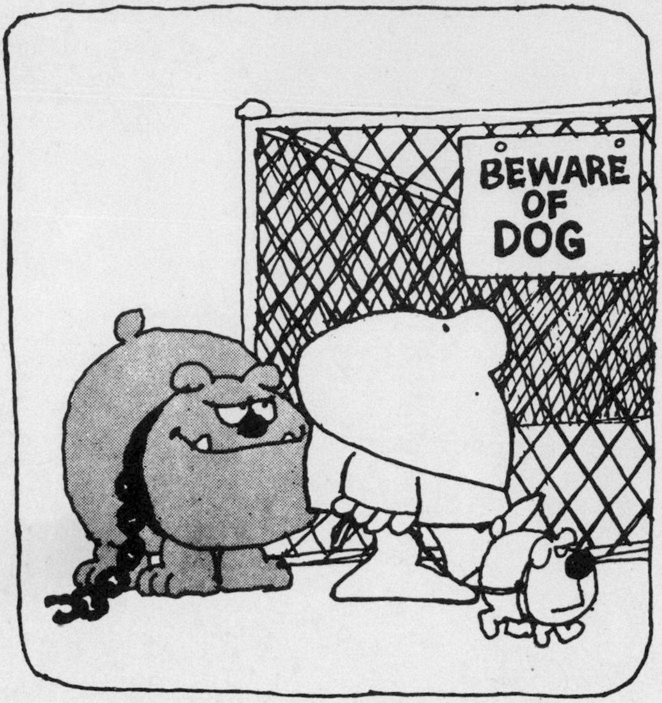
BEWARE
OF
DOG

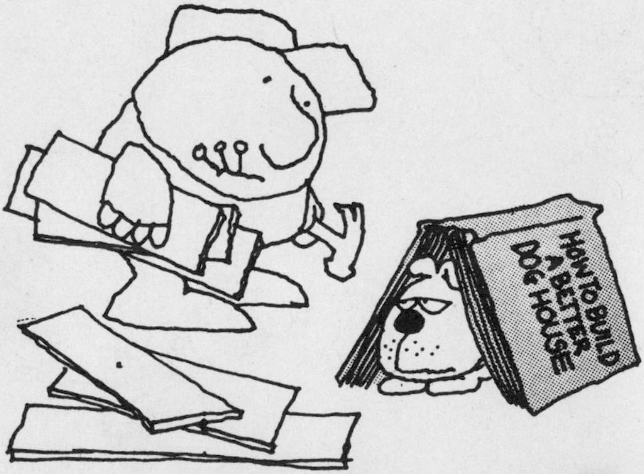
HOW TO BUILD
A BETTER
DOG HOUSE

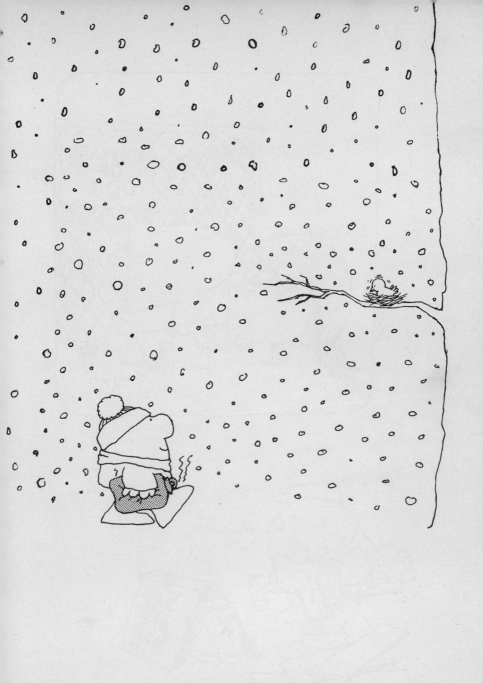

ZiGGY FaCES LiFe

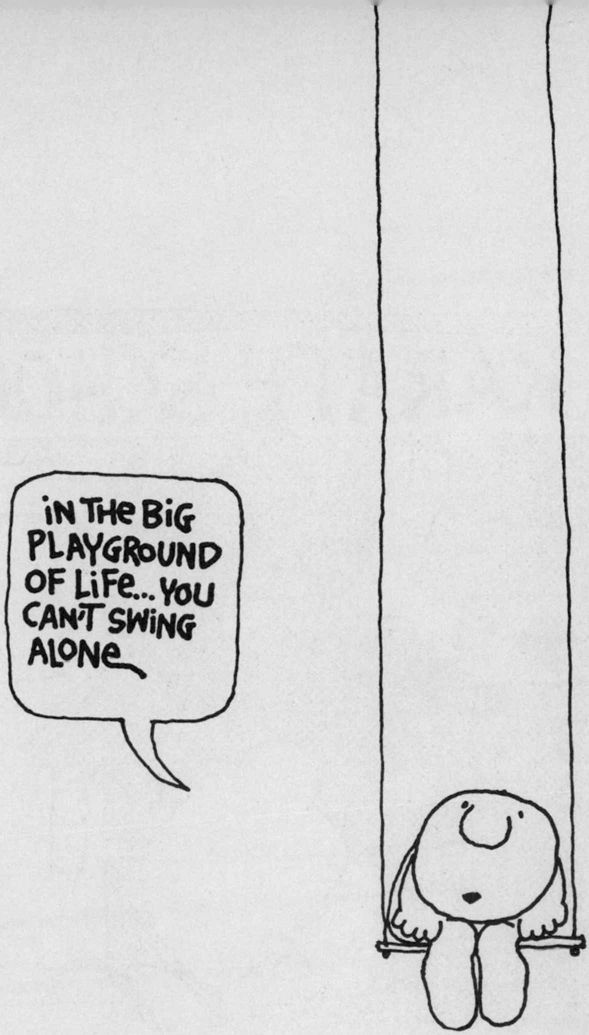
IN THE BIG PLAYGROUND OF LIFE... YOU CAN'T SWING ALONE

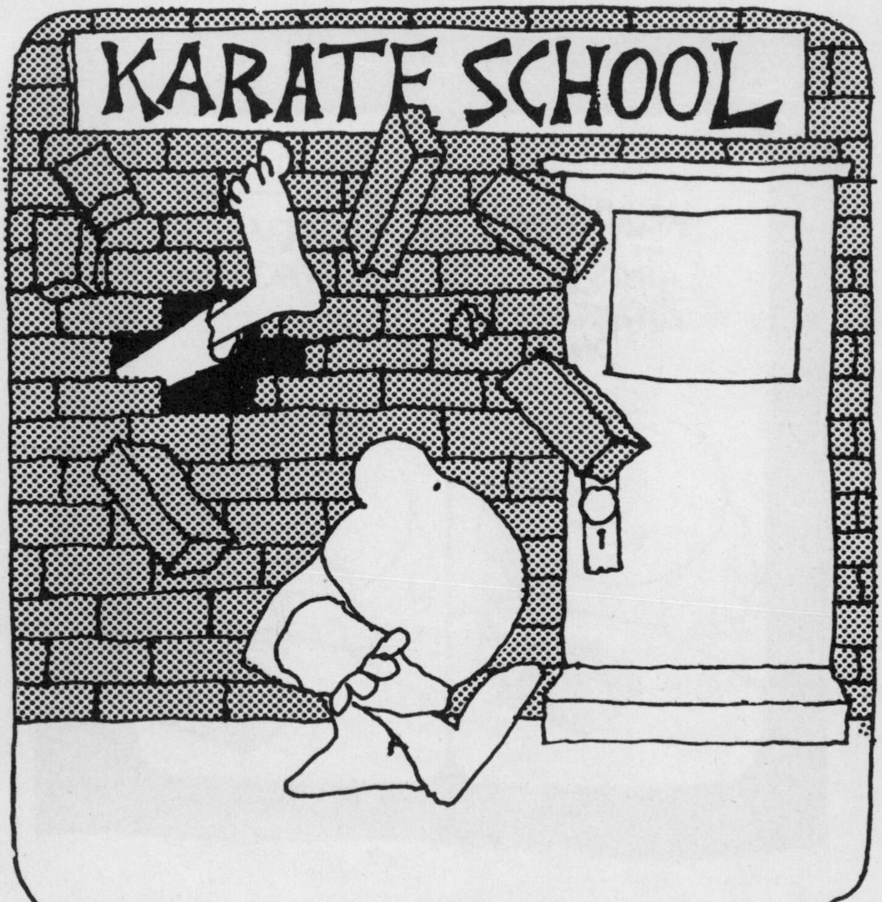
KARATE SCHOOL

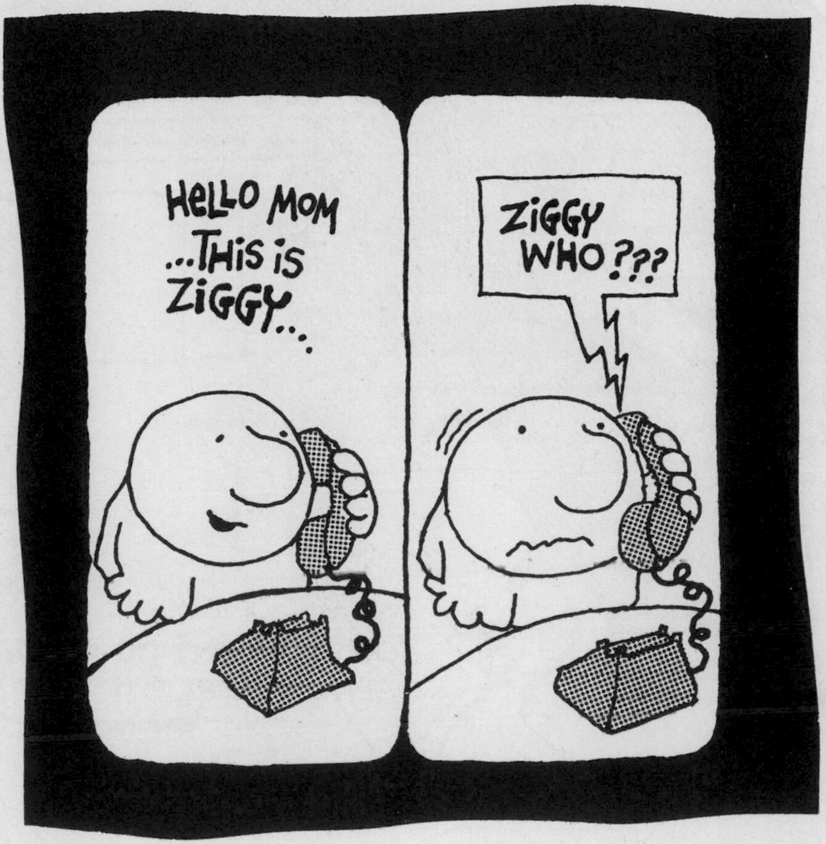
HELLO MOM ...THIS IS ZIGGY....
ZIGGY WHO???

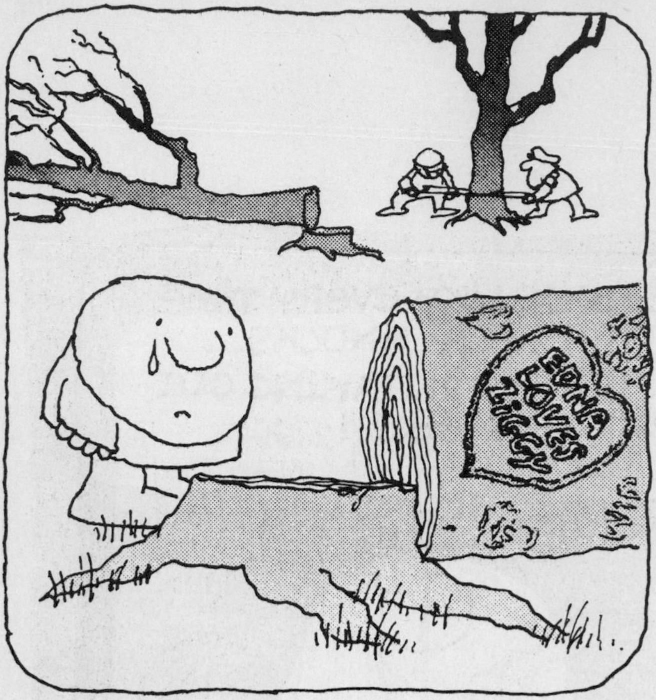
LOVES
ZIGGY

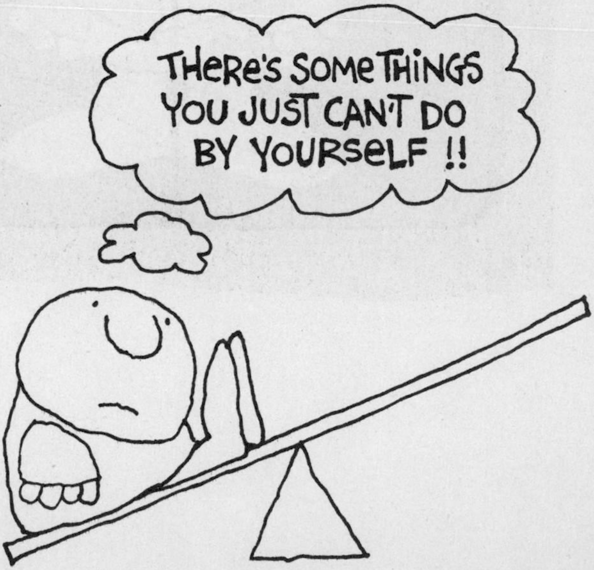
THERE'S SOME THINGS YOU JUST CAN'T DO BY YOURSELF !!

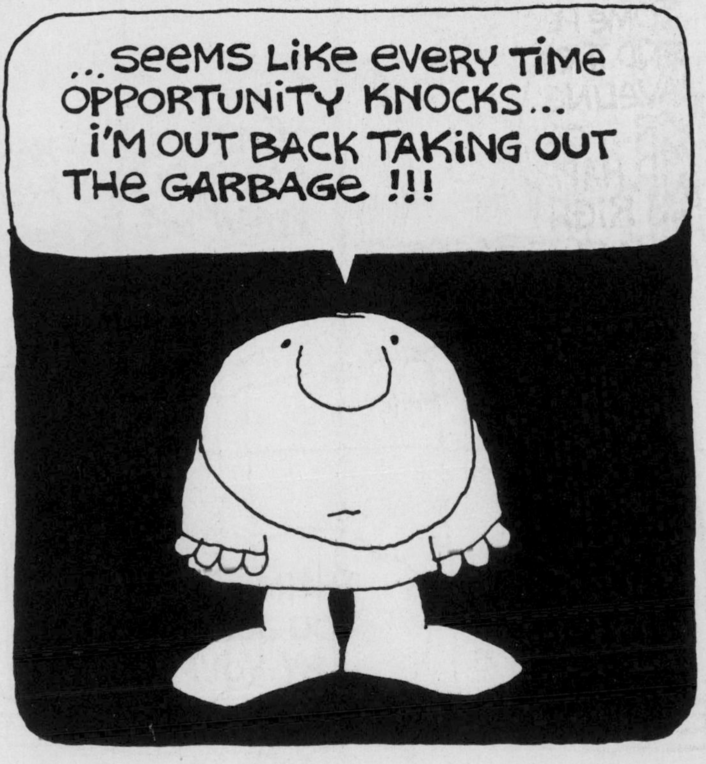
...SEEMS LIKE EVERY TIME OPPORTUNITY KNOCKS... I'M OUT BACK TAKING OUT THE GARBAGE !!!

SOME PEOPLE SPEND THEIR LIVES TRAVELING THE WORLD OVER... ONLY TO FIND, HAPPINESS LIES RIGHT IN THEIR OWN BACK YARD....
....MINE JUST HAS A BIG PUDDLE FROM LAST NIGHT'S RAIN !!

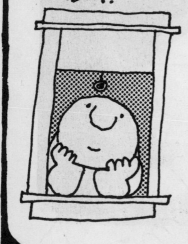

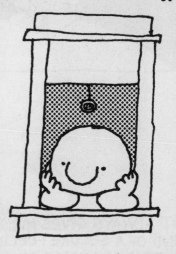

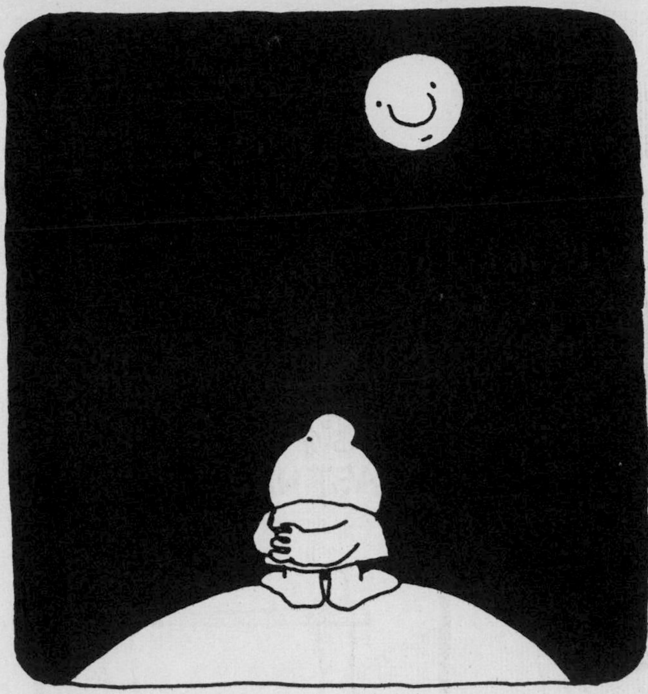

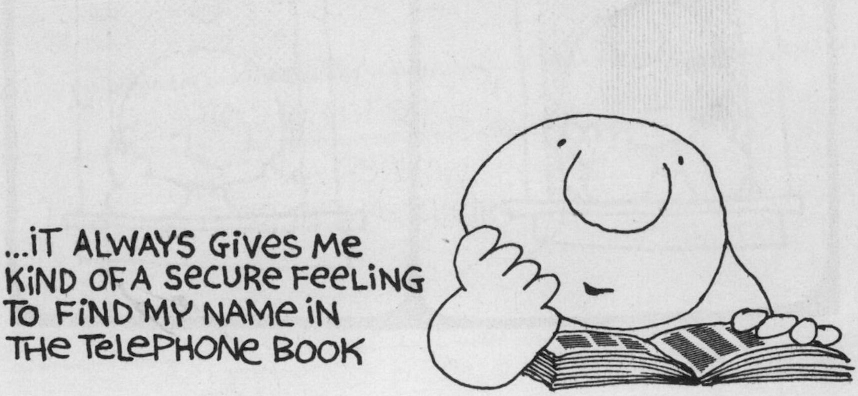
...IT ALWAYS GIVES ME
KIND OF A SECURE FEELING
TO FIND MY NAME IN
THE TELEPHONE BOOK

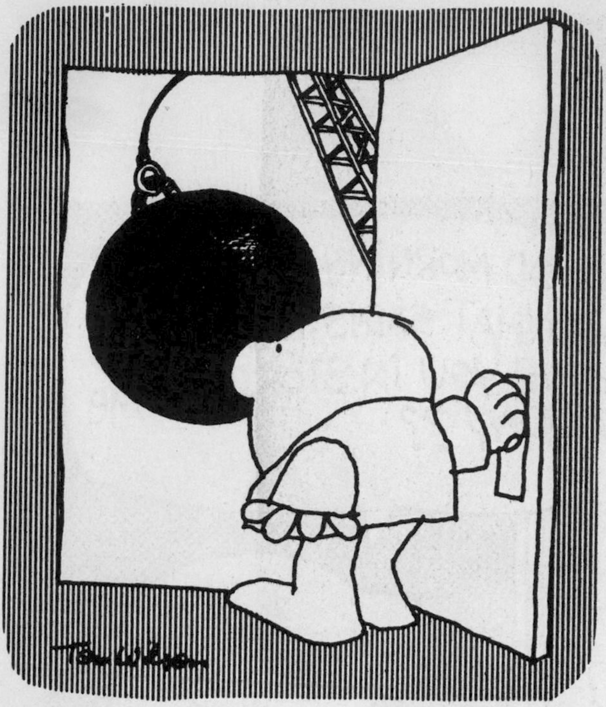

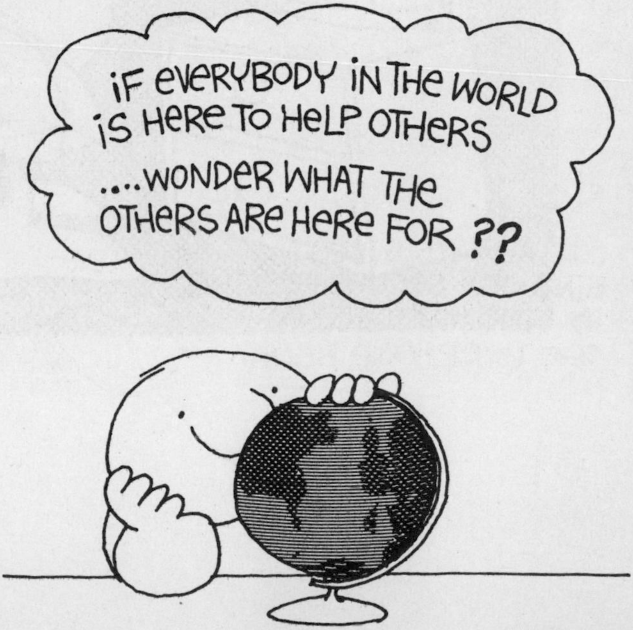
IF EVERYBODY IN THE WORLD IS HERE TO HELP OTHERS
....WONDER WHAT THE OTHERS ARE HERE FOR ??

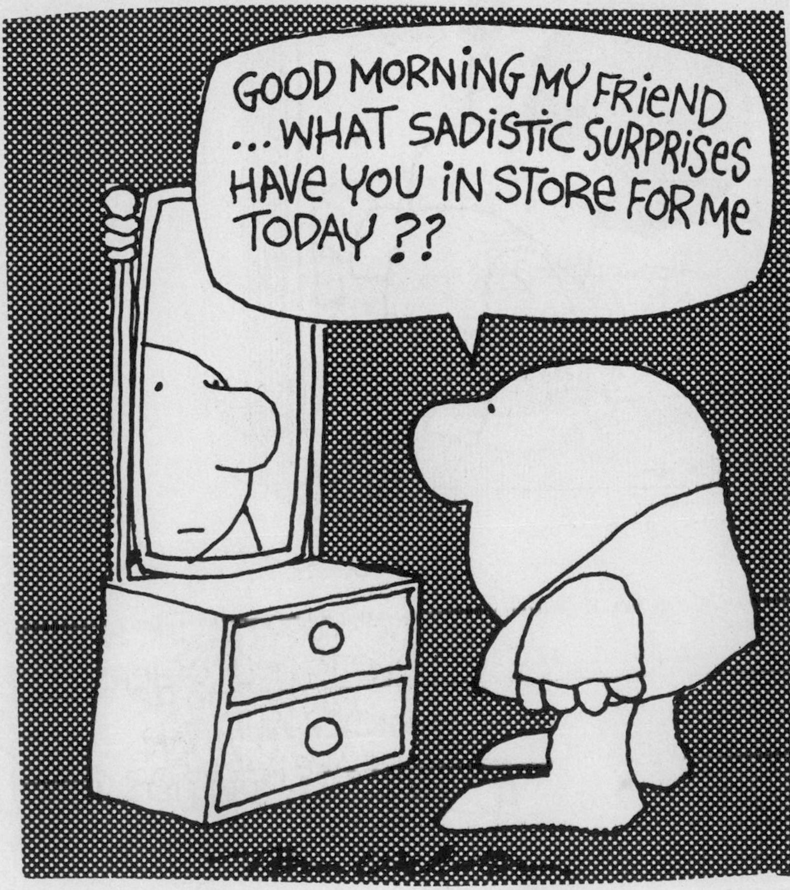
GOOD MORNING MY FRIEND ...WHAT SADISTIC SURPRISES HAVE YOU IN STORE FOR ME TODAY ??

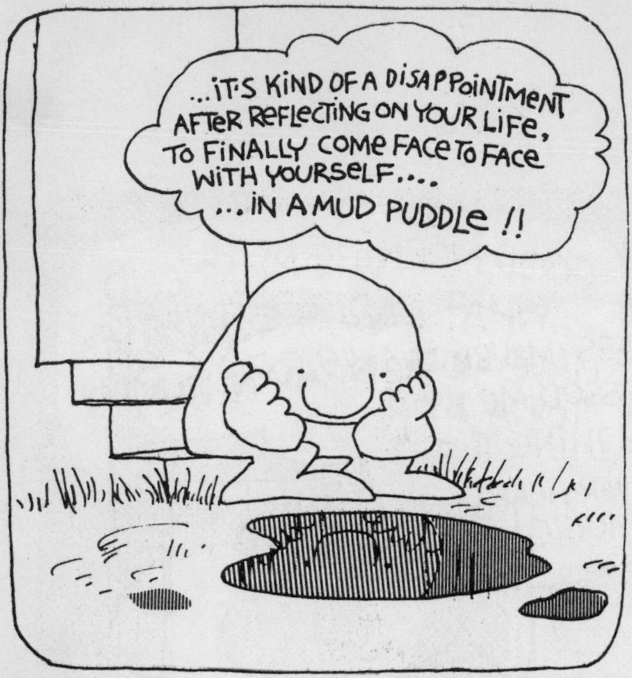
...IT'S KIND OF A DISAPPOINTMENT AFTER REFLECTING ON YOUR LIFE, TO FINALLY COME FACE TO FACE WITH YOURSELF.... ...IN A MUD PUDDLE !!

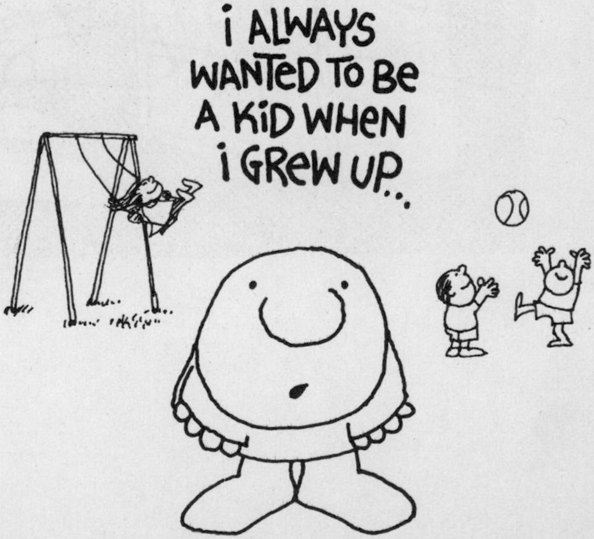
I ALWAYS WANTED TO BE A KID WHEN I GREW UP...

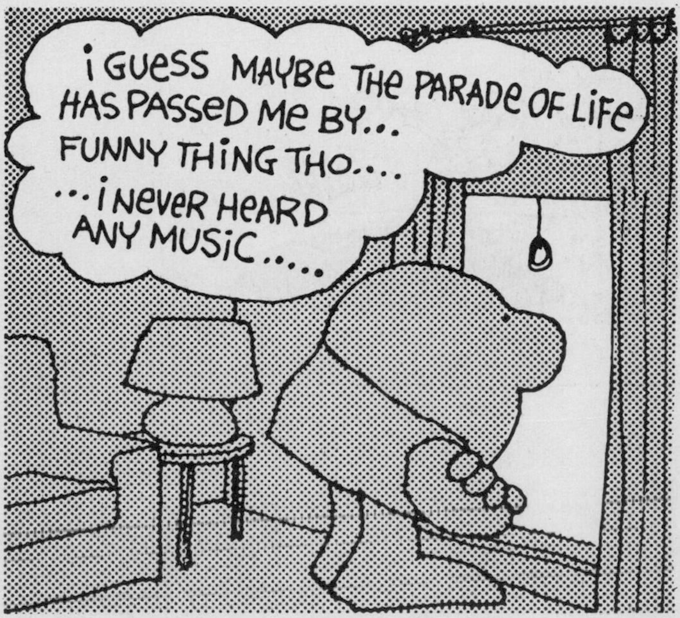

i GUESS MAYBE THE PARADE OF LIFE HAS PASSED ME BY... FUNNY THiNG THO.... ...i NEVER HEARD ANY MUSiC.....

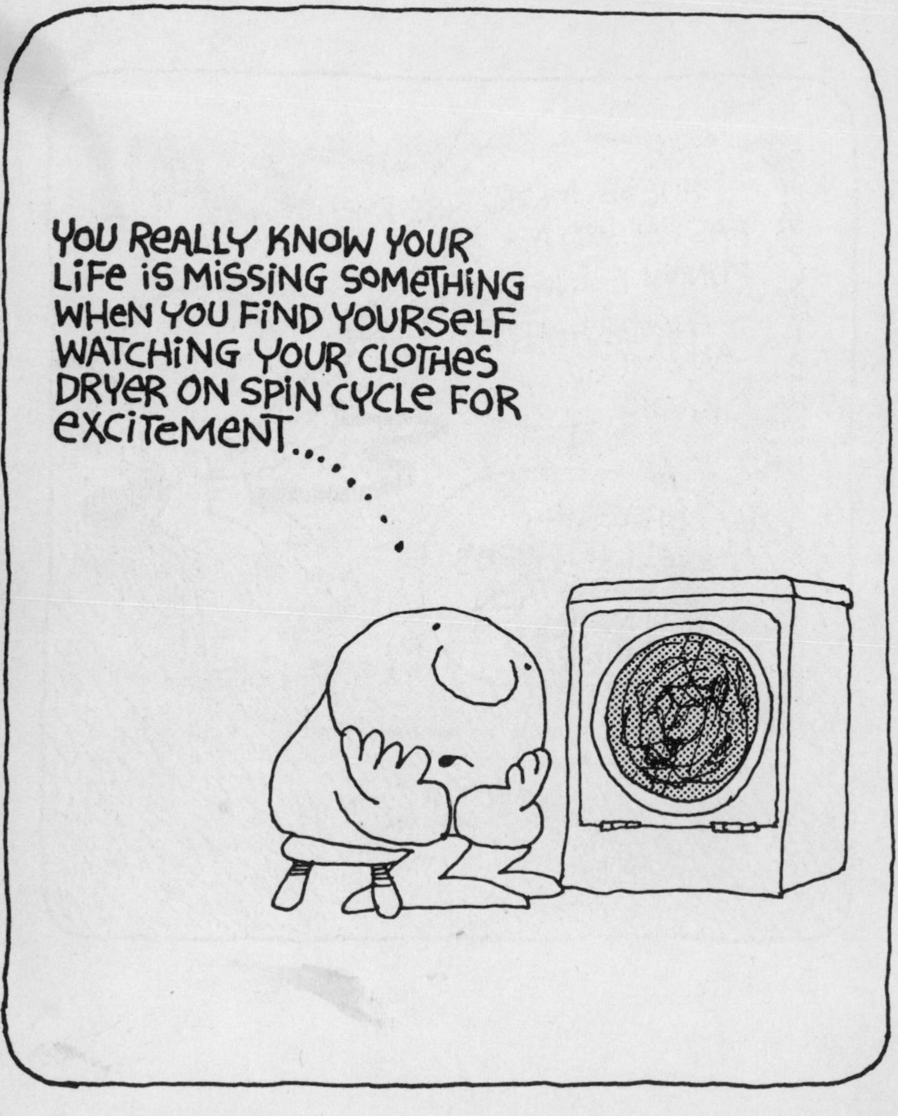
YOU REALLY KNOW YOUR LIFE IS MISSING SOMETHING WHEN YOU FIND YOURSELF WATCHING YOUR CLOTHES DRYER ON SPIN CYCLE FOR EXCITEMENT......

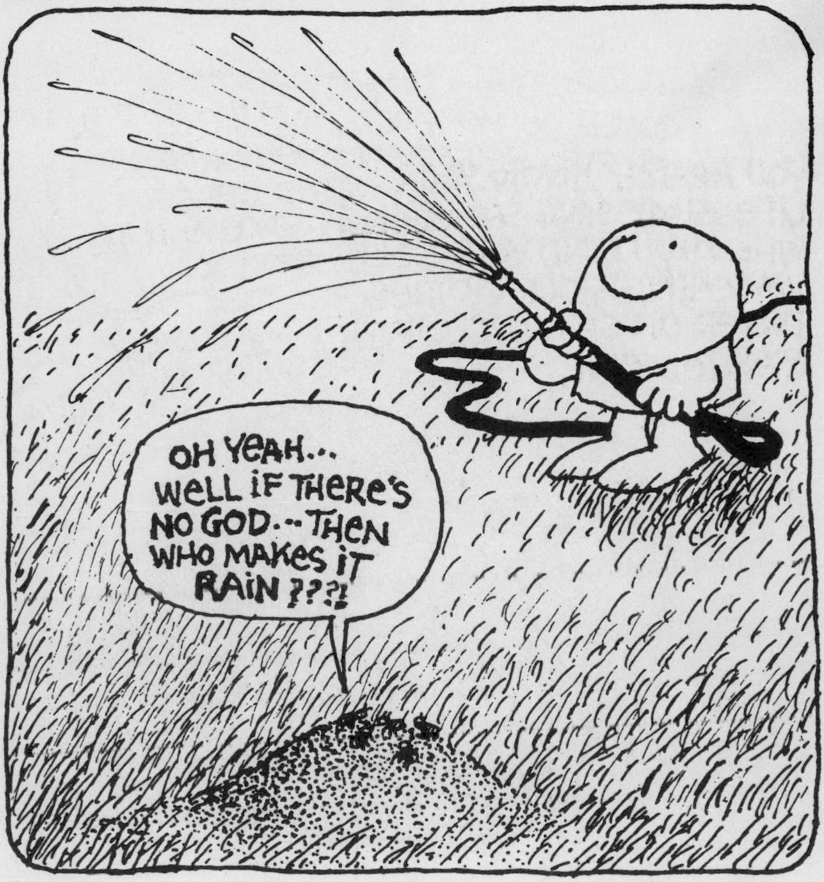
OH YEAH... WELL IF THERE'S NO GOD.-- THEN WHO MAKES IT RAIN ???!

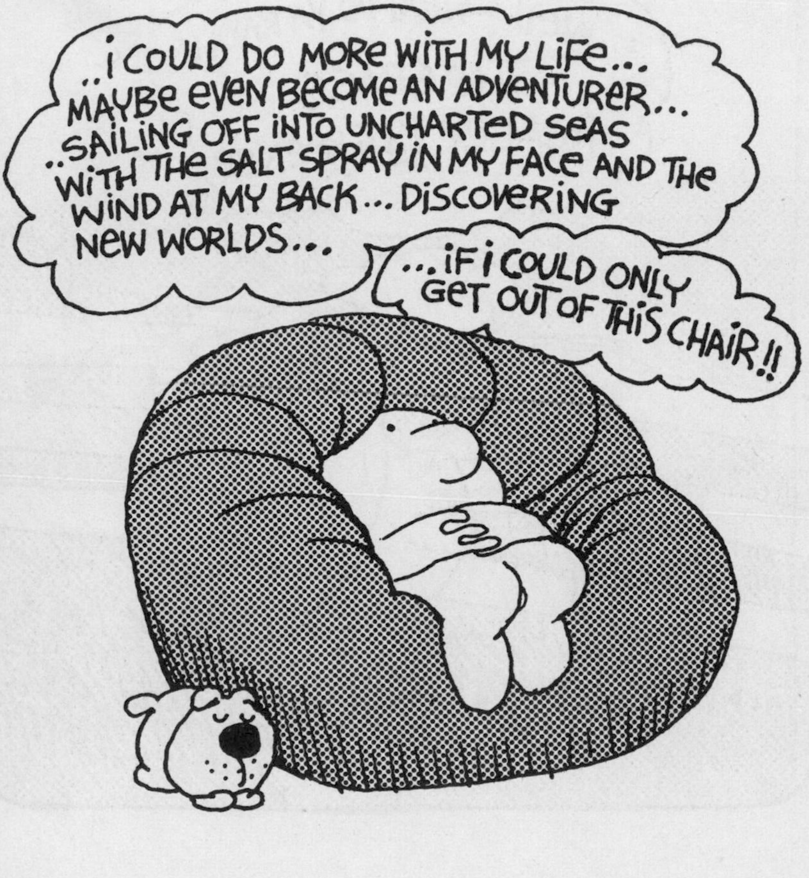
..i COULD DO MORE WITH MY LiFe... MAYBe eVEN BeCOMe AN ADVeNTURER... ..SAILING OFF INTO UNCHARTED SEAS ..WITH THE SALT SPRAY IN MY FACE AND THE WIND AT MY BACK... DISCOVERING NEW WORLDS...
...iF i COULD ONLY GET OUT OF THIS CHAIR!!

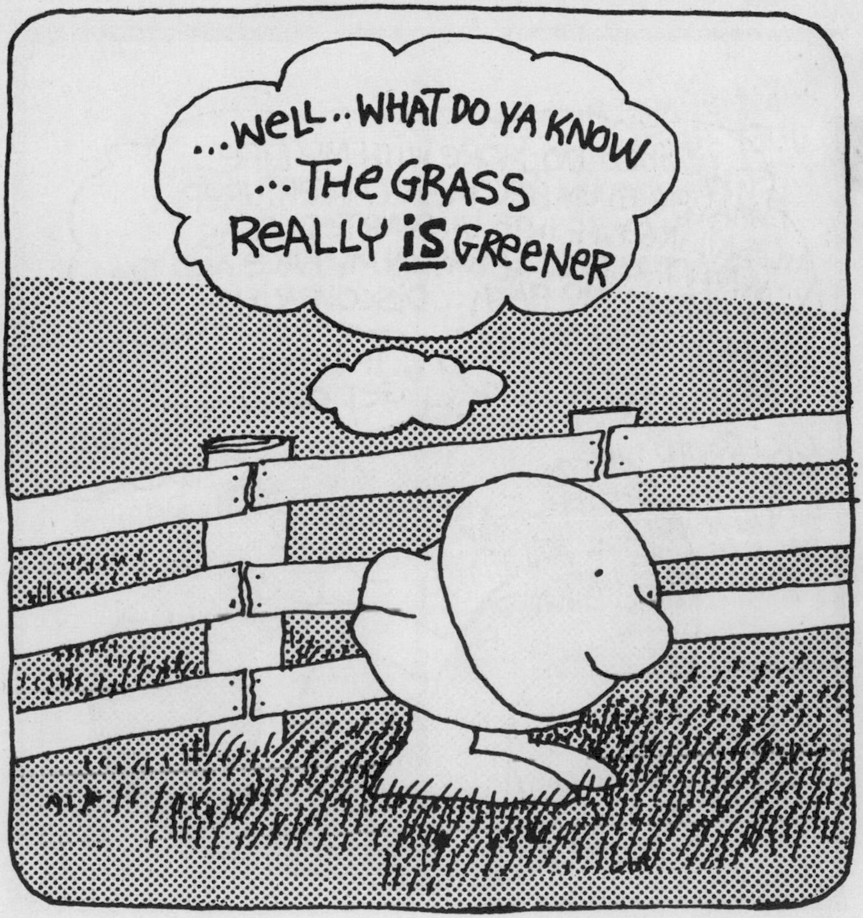
...WELL..WHAT DO YA KNOW
...THE GRASS
REALLY IS GREENER

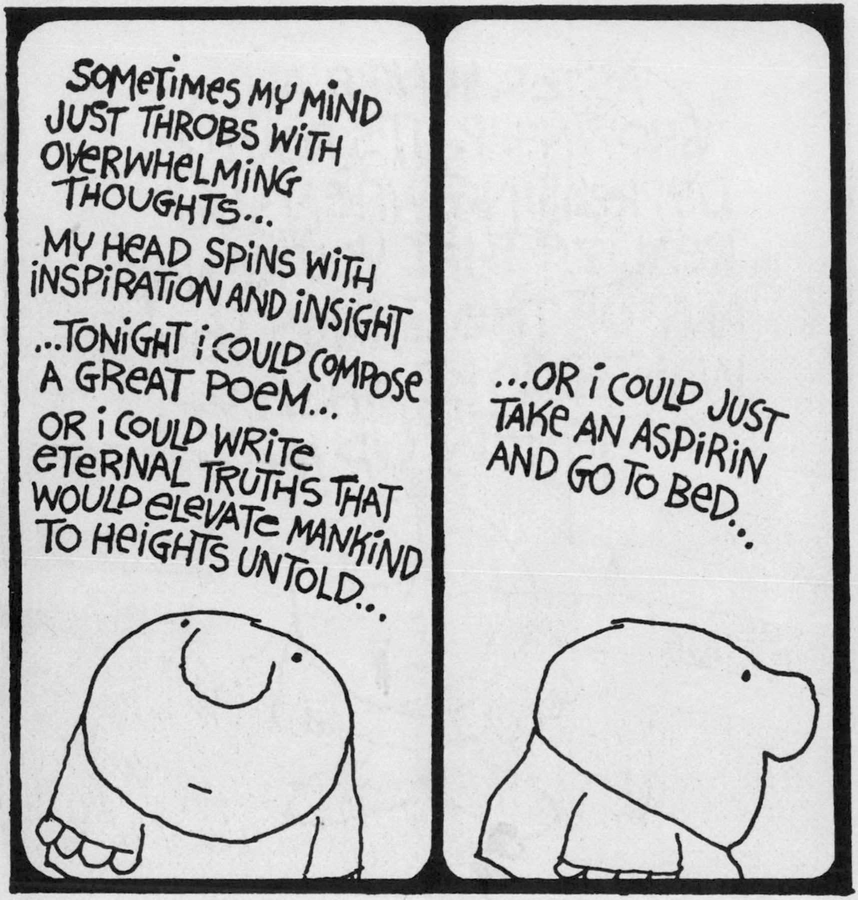
SOMETIMES MY MIND JUST THROBS WITH OVERWHELMING THOUGHTS...
MY HEAD SPINS WITH INSPIRATION AND INSIGHT
...TONIGHT I COULD COMPOSE A GREAT POEM...
OR I COULD WRITE ETERNAL TRUTHS THAT WOULD ELEVATE MANKIND TO HEIGHTS UNTOLD...
...OR I COULD JUST TAKE AN ASPIRIN AND GO TO BED...

AFTER YOU'RE ALL GROWN UP... IT'S REALLY DEPRESSING WHEN YOU REALIZE THAT YOU'RE NOT ANY OF THE THINGS YOU WANTED TO BE WHEN YOU GREW UP!!!

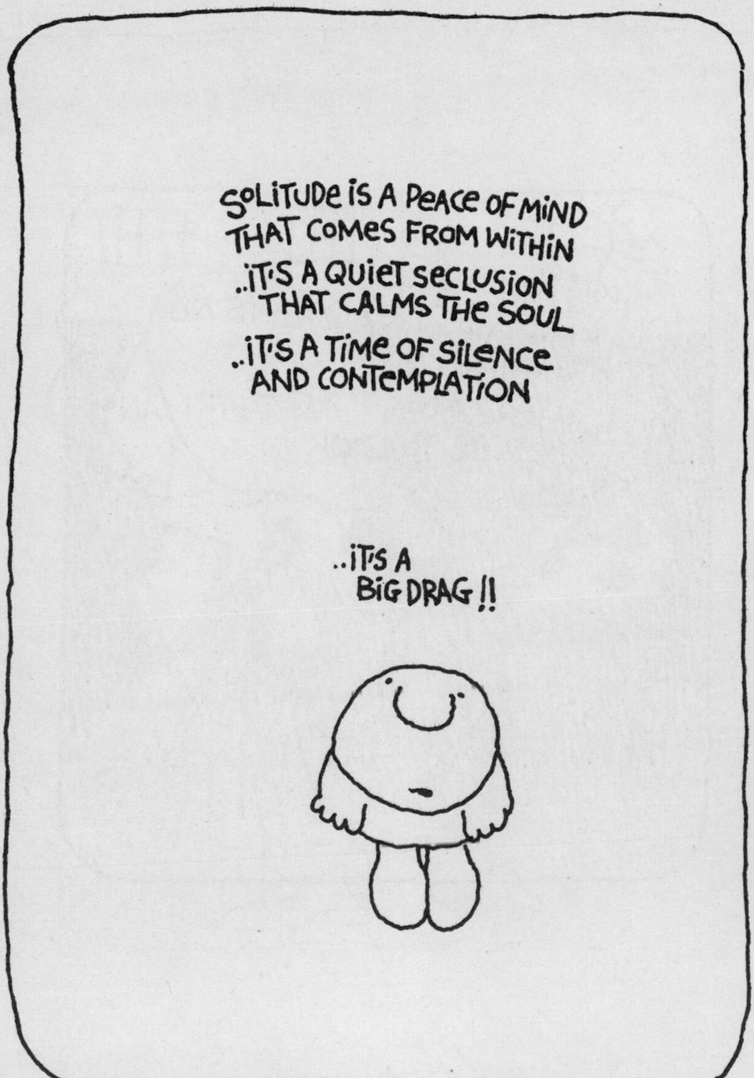
SOLITUDE IS A PEACE OF MIND THAT COMES FROM WITHIN
..IT'S A QUIET SECLUSION THAT CALMS THE SOUL
..IT'S A TIME OF SILENCE AND CONTEMPLATION
..IT'S A BIG DRAG !!

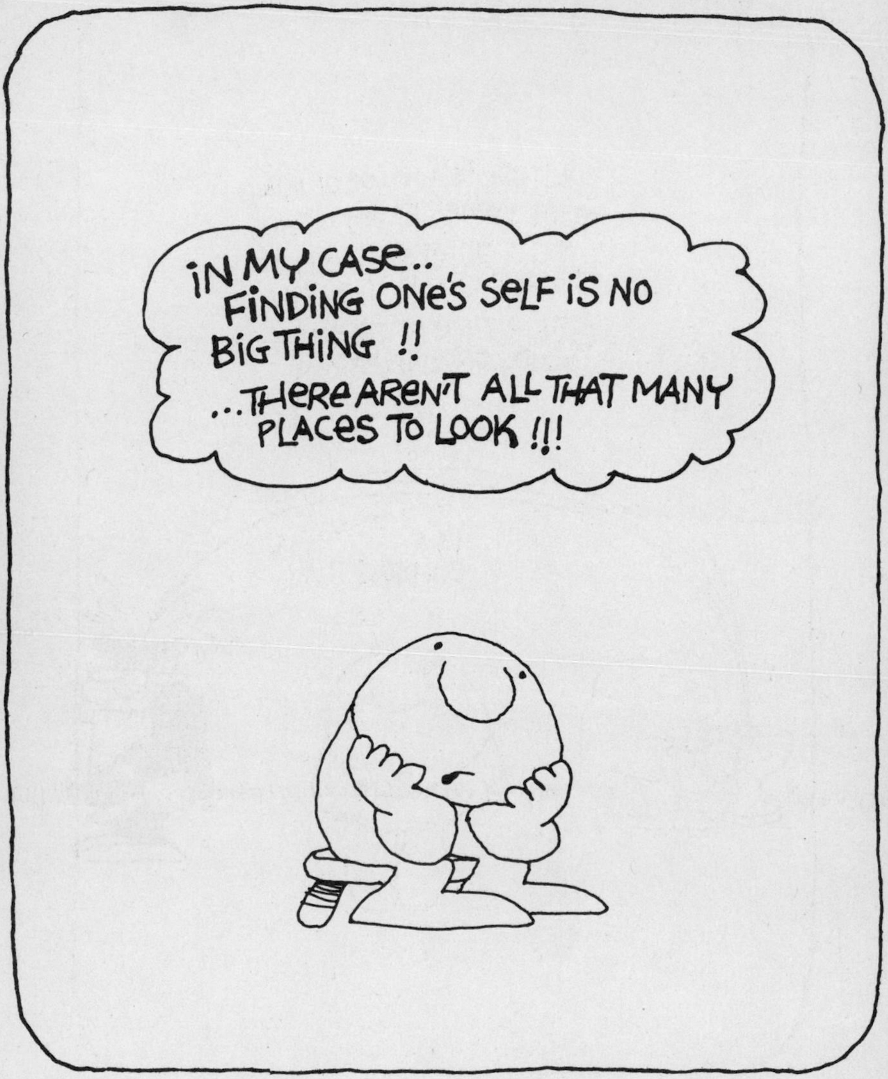
IN MY CASE..
FINDING ONE'S SELF IS NO
BIG THING !!
...THERE AREN'T ALL THAT MANY
PLACES TO LOOK !!!

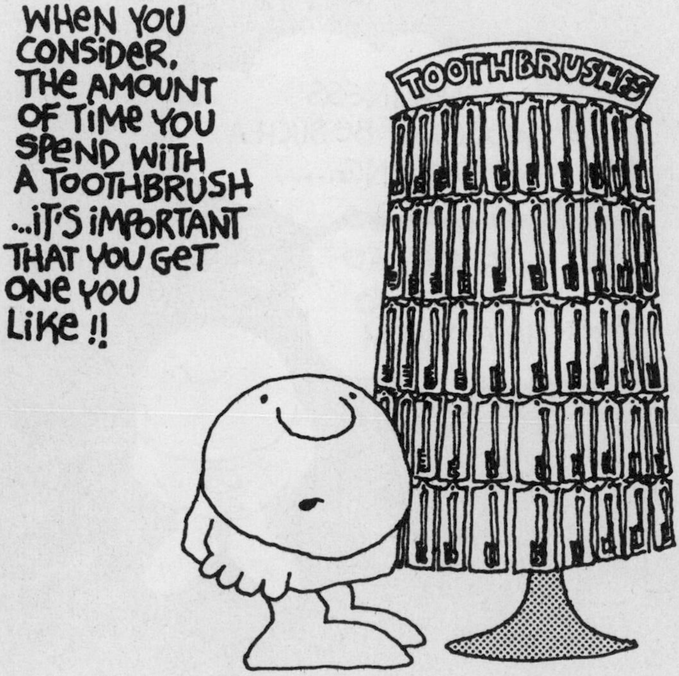
WHEN YOU CONSIDER, THE AMOUNT OF TIME YOU SPEND WITH A TOOTHBRUSH ...IT'S IMPORTANT THAT YOU GET ONE YOU LIKE !!
TOOTHBRUSHES

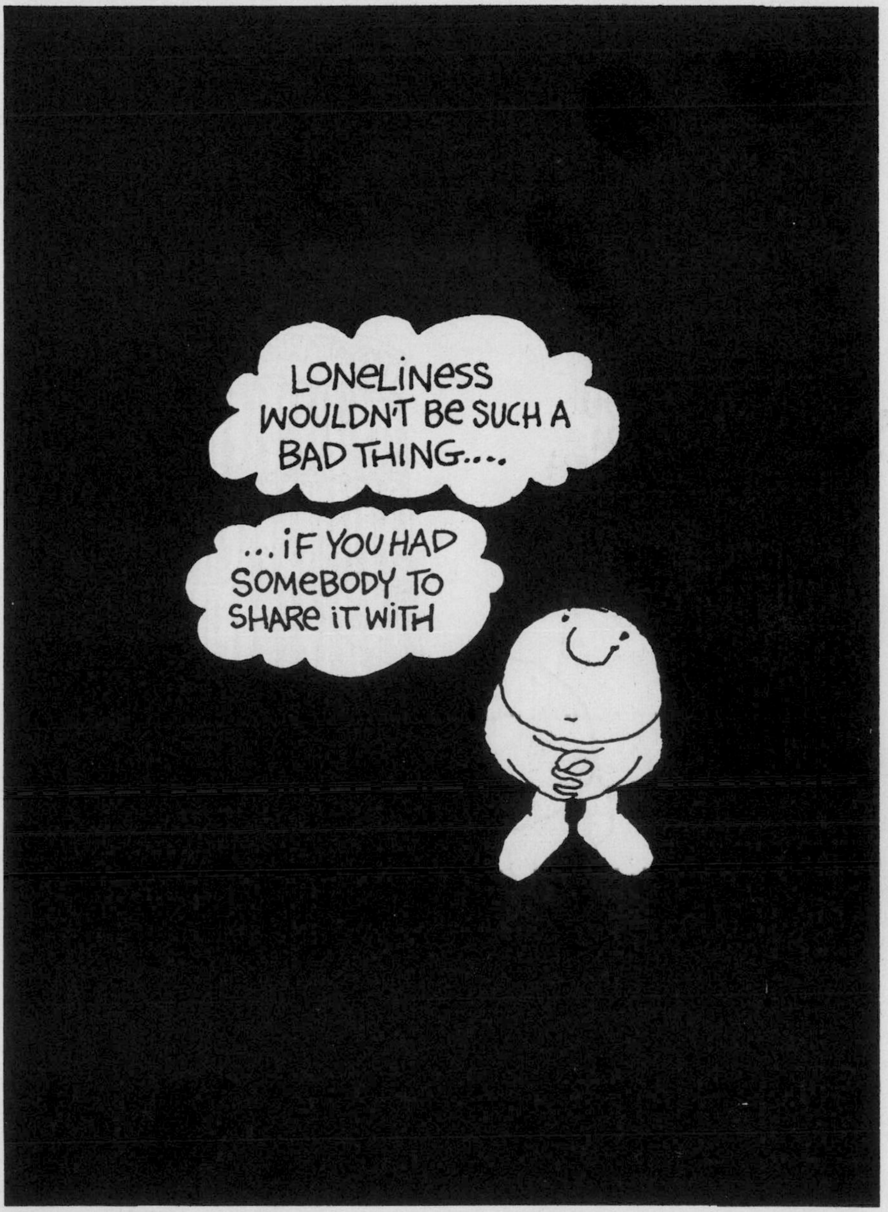
LONELINESS WOULDN'T BE SUCH A BAD THING....
...IF YOU HAD SOMEBODY TO SHARE IT WITH

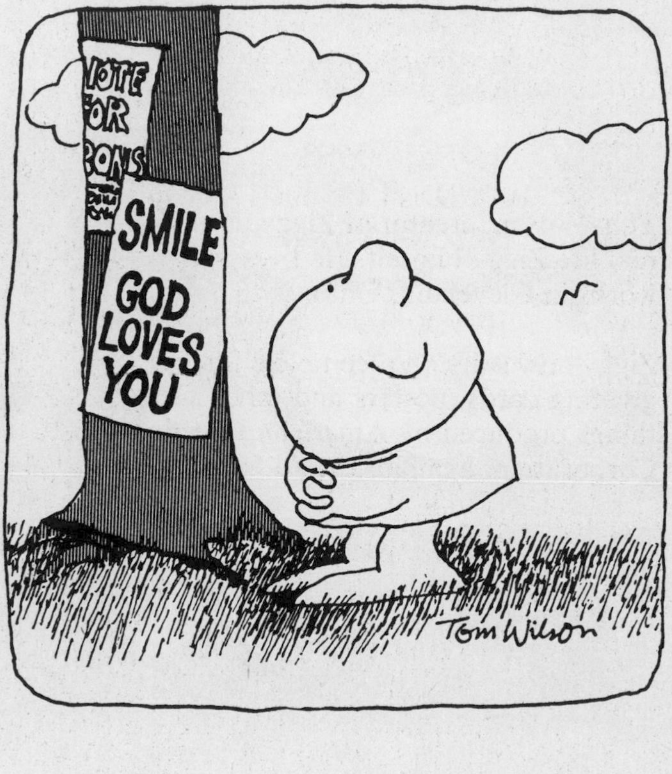
SMILE
GOD LOVES YOU
Tom Wilson

Tom Wilson, creator of Ziggy, is a
real-life Ziggy himself. He lives and
works in Cleveland, Ohio.

Ziggy now stars on a complete line of
greeting cards, posters and other such
things produced by American Greeting Card
Corporation, available at all fine stores.